How to avoid slimming

By Cliff Parker and available from New English Library:

HOW TO AVOID YOUR GARDEN
HOW TO AVOID FLYING
HOW TO AVOID SEX
HOW TO AVOID SLIMMING

How to avoid slimming

Cliff Parker

Illustrated by Barry Robson

NEW ENGLISH LIBRARY

A New English Library Original Publication, 1983

First New English Library Paperback Edition October 1983

NEL Books are published by
New English Library,
Mill Road, Dunton Green,
Sevenoaks, Kent.
Editorial office: 47 Bedford Square, London WC1B 3DP.

Made and printed in Great Britain by
Richard Clay (The Chaucer Press) Ltd, Bungay, Suffolk

Parker, Cliff
How to avoid slimming.
1. Reducing diet—Anecdotes, facetiae, satire, etc.
I. Title
613′.2′5 RM222.2

ISBN 0–450–05623–6

CONTENTS

CHAPTER ONE

Last Things First

At the risk of your putting this book back on the shelf, I'm giving the Message first instead of last.

Many books on slimming go through the whole rigmarole of calories, carbohydrates, fats, proteins, fibre, exercises, metabolic rates, fluids, heredity and Uncle Tom Cobbleigh and leave the secret of losing weight right until the end.

This leaves a lot of people disappointed, because they knew the secret already. As you do.

It's like the man in search of The Answer. He walked right across Europe, through the Balkans, across Bulgaria, right through Turkey, Iran, Afghanistan, India, Nepal, and finally into Tibet.

There he met the guru he had braved years of danger and hardship to meet.

'What is the Answer, Holy One?' he asked. 'What is the Meaning of Life?'

The old man told him: revealed the answer to the Great Mystery.

'My God!' said the disciple. 'I've walked through parching deserts and freezing blizzards to meet you. Five thousand long and dangerous miles in search of the Truth — and all you can say is, "Life is an artichoke"!'

. . . So, to save you having to journey right through to the back of the book to find the answer to the burning question 'Why am I overweight?', here it comes:

1. **You eat too much.**
2. **You don't move enough.**

That's all?

That's all.

What's all this about avoiding slimming? You can't lose weight by not slimming?

Yes, you can. Slimming is a conscious, often boring and debilitating drag, and slimmers often try to lose too much too soon. Any given method is seldom pursued to the end. And most slimmers put back the weight they've lost.

You get your weight down, at a healthy rate, and keep it down, by:

1. **Eating less.**
2. **Moving more.**

Too simple? Of course it's too simple. But peel away the leaves of the artichoke, and that's what you find at the centre. That's the basis of every slimming course and the message at the heart of every slimming book.

This is not to decry slimming clubs: good ones provide motivation, discipline and the therapy of knowing that others are in the same boat. But away from the club, temptation lies at home.

The purpose of this book is to take your mind off temptation. To give you something else to do instead of think about food. To help you laugh at a weight problem that otherwise might have you crying.

If nothing else, this book will put you off your grub. And by the end of it you could already have lost weight — if only by sweating it off in sheer fright.

CHAPTER TWO

Why Me?

So excess weight is caused by taking in more energy, i.e. food, than we use up.

But how come, you may ask, I eat less than the next man or woman and yet put on weight? And he or she eats more and stays as thin as a rail?

Assuming that he or she exercises no more than you, it's probably because they have a different metabolic rate: the rate at which the body burns up fuel. They're running all day with the choke out, using more fuel for the same mileage, and not having any left to lay up as fat.

So it's not just the *amount* of food you're eating that causes the trouble: it's that the amount, however meagre it seems to you, is *more* than your body needs to get through the day. Some people are just lucky, that's all.

Why do we eat — and drink — more than we need? Check your lifestyle and you'll probably come up with one of the following:

For Pleasure. It's nice. Grub's lovely. And there's nothing like a good vintage wine to go with it. And perhaps a glass of brandy afterwards. Or, particularly for men, a few drinks in the pub before you get home for the meal.

To Compensate. Food for many is a symbol or a substitute: for love, for security, for sex. If you're worried, tense, unhappy, broke, insecure — or just not getting your ration of passion — you can eat more without even realising it. Another prime cause is boredom: which is why this book hopes to lift you out of it, if it's only by shock therapy.

From Habit. Often the habits start in childhood. You've always been used to certain foods and you go on eating them, even though nowadays you're told time after time that they're the wrong ones.

Many overweight people claim their size is hereditary: one or both parents were big. And it is a fact that children of fat parents tend also to be fat because they've inherited the metabolism. But they've also inherited the eating habits — and those they *can* do something about.

Perhaps your work routine includes breaks in which you automatically open a packet of biscuits or sandwiches to go with the coffee or tea. Not that you eat a lot: just enough to see you through till lunchtime.

On holiday you'll go for the traditional ice creams, candy floss — makes you feel like a kid again — and a blow-out or two as a special treat. A trip to the theatre probably includes a box of chocolates, drinks at the interval and a meal afterwards as a matter of routine.

* * *

A British nutritionist has said that the best way to lose weight is *slowly*, with a varied diet, eating a bit more fibre and a bit less food. Slow slimming is the surest, giving the body time to adjust and with a much better chance of the weight reduction being permanent.

A varied diet ensures that you take in the three essentials:

Nutrients. The raw materials which build and repair your body. These are: proteins, carbohydrates, fats, vitamins, minerals and water.

Energy. This provides the power for the body to carry out its tasks.

Fibre. Once known as roughage. Found in many vegetables and cereals.

All contain *calories*, to one degree or another. Calories are units of heat used to measure energy — a teaspoonful of sugar gives enough to boil two pints of water — and any calories which are not used go to lay up fat in the body.

It's calories we want to cut down. At one time it was also carbohydrates, but that old bogy has been laid by several nutritional bodies, including the British Royal College of Physicians.

Cutting down on carbohydrates such as potatoes and bread, it said in a 1983 report on obesity, is 'nutritionally and medically inappropriate,' and went on:

'There is increasing evidence that fibre-rich starchy foods are important components of the diet. Carbohydrates are not uniquely fattening.'

It advised the overweight to increase their consumption of cereals and brown bread, together with fruit and vegetables. Food rich in fats, such as meat products and fried foods, along with foods containing a lot of sugar, should be cut down.

So to lose weight you either have to cut down on the calories you're taking in, or increase your physical exertions to burn them off. The sensible thing is to do both, remembering that it takes a lot of exercise to shift a modest amount of fat.

There is an enormous difference between calorie needs. A man doing heavy manual work needs about 3,500 a day, a male office worker about 2,500, and a female office worker about 2,200. (Remember, too, that these groups are only stereotypes: one manual worker may need more or fewer calories than the man working next to him.)

It takes only 3,500 spare calories to lay up a pound of body fat — so by going just 500 calories over the top every day without compensatory exercise, you could be almost 14lb heavier at the end of three months. You'd have to walk an extra mile a day for a year to lose 10lb of that. But think: if you walked that extra mile a day and hadn't eaten more — you'd have lost 10lb in 12 months without eating less.

Most of us in the West are eating more than we should, so providing you're eating a *varied* diet, you don't have to worry about going short of proteins, vitamins or minerals. About the only people likely to suffer from nutrient deficiency — apart from its occasional and natural occurrence in pregnancy — are fussy feeders and crash dieters. Because of the amount of animal foods in our diet — meat, fish, milk, cheese and eggs — we're eating about twice as much protein as we need.

Foods to cut down on are those high in calories in the forms of sugar, alcohol and fat.

Sugar has no value except as a source of energy, which is supplied by other foods anyway, yet the average British adult takes in 95lb of the stuff in a year. (As well as in the obvious cakes, pastries and sweets, it's in all sorts of things such as the syrups of tinned fruits, ice creams and sweetened drinks.) In that annual intake of sugar are enough calories to fuel the body for a 2,000-mile walk. So if you want to make it easy on your feet, cut out sugar.

Alcoholic drinks are frighteningly high in calories, and the cause of many a would-be slimmer's downfall because of their added effect of weakening the will. Pity.

Fat — in meat, dairy products, chocolates and fried foods — is not only high in calories: it encourages the build-up of fat-like deposits in the blood vessels which can eventually clog them and lead to heart disease. Chicken, turkey and white fish, however, are low in fat. So are *some* dairy products such as skimmed milk, low-fat yogurt and cottage cheese. (*Cottage* cheese: all others have a high fat content.) Vegetable fats — with the exceptions of palm and coconut oil — are not as harmful as animal fats, but they are still rich in calories and best left alone.

* * *

Britain's Health Education Council is campaigning hard for people to lose weight and to exercise. It has simplified the whole calorie-counting business — often the reason slimmers give up a diet — by producing the *Traffic Light Guide to Staying Slim,* reproduced below.

The main sorts of food are divided into three groups according to their calorie concentration. RED is high in calories, AMBER medium, and GREEN low. Even small quantities of the RED group foods contain as many calories as quite large helpings of GREEN group foods.

It doesn't mean you must never touch the Reds — just remember that a little goes a long way.

Red — stop and think
Sugar, sweets, chocolate, cakes, pies, sweet pastries, biscuits, heavy puddings, honey, syrup, treacle, jam, marmalade, fruit tinned in syrup, cream, butter, margarine, lard, cooking oil, fat on meat, salad dressing, salad cream or mayonnaise, chips, crisps, peanuts.

Amber — go carefully
Fatty meats (like bacon or salami), sausages, liver pâté, eggs, milk, oily fish (like herring, mackerel, sardines, tuna, salmon), cheese (except cottage cheese), thick creamy soups, nuts, bread (white or wholemeal), rice, pasta (like spaghetti and macaroni), savouries. Wines, beer and cider. Aperitifs, spirits and liqueurs. Most soft drinks and mixers.

Green — go right ahead
Fresh fruit, salads, green and root vegetables including potatoes (not fried), white fish, seafood, poultry, game, lean meat, kidneys, cottage cheese, yogurt (natural), skimmed milk, bran, wholegrain cereals, clear soups. Low-calorie soft drinks, coffee and tea (without sugar), water.

CHAPTER THREE

A Lot of it About

Overweight? You're not on your own and you're not a freak. There's a lot of it about. Which is not to say you can sit back and do nothing about it. To help put you off your grub here are:

Some Sobering Thoughts

★ One quarter of the world's population — i.e. the affluent developed countries — eats three quarters of the world's food. Which explains why obesity is not a problem in the Third World.

★ Eighty million Americans — out of a population of around 210 million — are overweight.

★ Thirty per cent of British adults and five per cent of children are overweight.

★ In Europe and the USA, one man in five and one woman in three are *20 per cent* over the desirable weight.

★ At any given time in America, 20 million people are trying to lose weight, and every year up to four books on slimming get into the top 10 bestsellers list.

★ Two out of every three British women and one out of every three men are on a diet.

★ The total weight of the British population is 3½ million tons — half a million tons of which is surplus fat.

★ Every year in Britain, obesity takes up 600,000 doctor-hours and costs the National Health Service £3 million in appetite-suppressant drugs.

★ Up to the age of 40, fewer women than men are overweight, but after that they seem to give up the struggle. From the age of 40 more than half the British, of both sexes, are too fat. Between 40 and 49, 60 per cent of men are over the top, but the women overtake them in the 50–59 age group with a staggering 65 per cent.

★ Only five per cent of dieters manage to sustain their weight loss.

★ A British survey of slimmers showed that Miss Average Slimmer is 5ft 5in tall, weighs 11st 9lb and has 2st 9lb to lose. She is 35 years old, with measurements of 39-31-42. More than 80 per cent of those interviewed said their problem was caused mainly by a sweet tooth and nibbling between meals, with alcohol mentioned frequently as a diet-breaker. More than half the women had carried around the excess weight, the equivalent of 18½ 2lb bags of sugar — or 18½ 2lb bags of anything — for five years.

Some Frightening Facts

★ A man who is 30 per cent overweight shortens his expected lifespan by 42 per cent. Women, who are less prone to heart disease, have their lifespans shortened by 30 per cent. Even only 10 per cent of surplus weight can cause an average lifespan reduction of 13 per cent for men, 10 per cent for women.

★ A British survey said that one in five 29-year-olds could die before they are 50. The causes are smoking, high fat diet, lack of exercise, obesity and the Pill — i.e., three out of the five causes attributable to eating and sitting.

★ Overweight people are more likely to suffer from — wait for it — heart attacks, strokes, high blood pressure, shortage of breath, varicose veins, foot trouble, chest trouble, backache, arthritis, diabetes and gallstones. Excess weight can also affect fertility, pregnancies and childbirth and cause complications after an operation.

* * *

Though obesity is a major problem of the Western world, it doesn't stop there.

The Soviet newspaper *Izvestia* attacked the excess weight carried by Russia's top people and the unsuccessful efforts of Moscow's Institute of Nutrition at fighting the flab.

The Institute does not slim people for money, as do health farms in the West, but studies diet, metabolism and slimming methods purely in the interests of science.

According to *Izvestia*, however, the slimming methods advocated — based on research by 200 staff specialists — are little short of fraudulent.

Over six years, 117 diet and slimming projects were carried out at a cost of nearly £8m. The only result was a report, the slimmest thing in the place, repeating obvious principles which the Institute had laid down a quarter of a century earlier.

Expensive imported equipment was lying around unused. One foreign machine, bought at a cost of several thousand roubles, had been used for only seven hours in five years.

Clients of the Institute, said *Izvestia,* were either influential people who had grown fat, or fat people who had grown influential. They flocked to the Institute in the hope of losing up to 50lb a month but, according to the newspaper, flocked out again not a lot thinner.

The best way for them to lose weight, the paper went on, would be for them to stop indulging themselves and drink a lot less.

Izvestia did give the Institute credit for one good slimming aid. The kitchens, it said, were so filthy that any patient seeing them would stop eating on the spot.

* * *

In Czechoslovakia, obesity among men has more than doubled in the past 15 years, matching a growth in the sales of food, alcohol and television sets. It would be reasonable to conclude that the Czech male is turning into a decadent Western-type slob: eating a big meal, then settling down with a few cans of booze to watch the telly. The moral being: No check on the weight means more weight on the Czech.

* * *

The world's fattest population is that of the tiny island of Nauru in the Central Pacific.

With an area of only 8.2 square miles and a circumference of 12 miles, it is the world's smallest nation. But because of its phosphate deposits, it is also the richest per head. And the fattest per body.

In the absence of much else to do, most of the 4,600 Nauruans eat about six pounds of rice and fish a day, and with other bits and pieces manage to notch up a daily 6,000 calories. Nobody looks twice at 12-year-old girls weighing 15 stone. Not that anybody wants to.

There are just a couple of snags. Diabetes, brought on by over-indulgence, is rife. The official figure is 42 per cent of the adult population, but other estimates put it as high as 90 per cent. And the average life expectancy is around 45.

Pity. Just when they were enjoying themselves.

* * *

The ultimate capitalist solution to obesity can be found in Fat City, USA — officially, Durham, North Carolina — where the town's university medical school is using a salt-free diet of rice and fruit that achieves sensational results.

The diet, says the university, is 'uneasy'. Which is medical talk for 'Bleargh!' or 'Eeeuch!' But it drains away fluid like an emptying bath at the rate of 2lb a day.

Every week tons of human flesh flop out of cars and buses to be swilled away. The average weight loss target is 10½ stone. The real star patients arrive at anything between 40 and 50 stone, hoping to lose the equivalent of two normal human beings.

Fat City is the last hope of the no-hopers. 'Slim or die', most of them have been told by their local doctors. Often it's the last hope because they can't afford to do it twice: the average cost of treatment is £2,000.

The university's initial and detailed examination costs from £450 to £600. Treatment costs £75 a week. Meals (meals!) run up another £26 a week. And rents for the town's smallest bedsits — in which many of the patients can barely stand up or turn around — start at £30 a week.

A few months of that and if you're not slim, your wallet certainly is.

* * *

There are dangers in losing too much weight too fast. You bruise easier, for a start, because the small blood vessels have been used to support from the fat around them. Once the fat goes the capillaries just sort of flop around and, until they've had time to get their strength back, tend to burst at the slightest bump.

Crash diets can leave you weak and ill, perhaps short of essential vitamins or minerals. Diets which involve getting rid of body fluids — often low-liquid diets with no fruit or vegetables — can damage your kidneys. What's more, the weight lost is water — and it goes straight back on with your first post-diet drink.

There's also the problem of clothes. You may not be able to afford a smaller outfit straight away, or may not even have noticed that you need one.

Newly-slim women, after executing some dashing Spanish-type swivels in the *paso doble* at the firm's dance, may find themselves awarded the novelty prize. Simply because when they swivelled one way, the strapless, backless dress swivelled another. Letting it all hang out. Others may have slimmed so far as to qualify for a couple of spot prizes.

Newly-slim men may find themselves standing up at a meeting, taking a deep breath to start the important speech — and being greeted with thunderous applause because their trousers are lying around their ankles. Many a newly-slim stand-up comic has discovered a knockout start to his act like this, followed by a season's booking for *No Sex, Please — We're British.*

The lack of awareness of how little flesh one is carrying can have even more serious effects. Scotland Yard's missing persons file is full of people who pulled the plug *before* stepping out of the bath. In areas where slimming clubs proliferate, local councils are fitting mesh screens to the drains in the hope of picking up a few stragglers. In the same areas, vacuum cleaner salesmen are offering models in which the bag can be opened from the inside.

* * *

Surely there must be *some* advantages to being fat? Of course there are.

In fact there are people about who are proud to be fat, and are campaigning for fairer deals for the overweight.

In Japan, 500 fatties formed the Great Japan Fat People's League. Among the attractions were a fat fashion show, fat athletics (presumably not *too* athletic), and a trip to Europe — with two seats reserved on the plane for each passenger.

Fat Lib and Fat Pride organisations have been started in America. In their support, a doctor wrote a book entitled *Fat is Beautiful*. The message was spoiled a bit by the fact that the book included a diet programme.

But what *are* the advantages of being fat?

Plump teenage girls tend to marry earlier than their slimmer sisters. Nobody's yet worked out whether it's because they're more attractive or that they grab the first chance that comes along.

Should you accidentally bump into somebody, it's usually you who stay upright. OK, they can sue for the extra damage occasioned by hitting the ground, but are you to blame for gravity?

If you're stuck on a mountain in a freezing blizzard, you are more likely to survive because your fat will keep you warm and nourish you until help arrives. Plus the fact that the rescue party has a better chance of seeing you, providing they don't mistake your inert form for a rocky outcrop.

If you fall off a cruise liner in mid-ocean, all you need do is tread water. You can keep warm long cnough to give the ship time to turn round and come back. Keep out of its path, though. Remember the *Titanic*.

The same applies if you're shipwrecked. You are less prone to exposure and can live off your blubber. Unless you are eyed by skinnier fellow-survivors who might think it better if *they* lived off your blubber.

There don't appear to be many other advantages, but at least it's a start. If you're a plump teenage girl with a habit of bumping into people, getting stuck on mountains and falling off ships, you've got a lot going for you.

* * *

Regular weighing shows whether fat is creeping up on you, and there's a right and a wrong way of doing it.

Use the same scales each time. And no cheating. No adjusting the gauge to show 7lb under.

Weigh yourself only once a week. No sense in panicking once a day.

Keep to the same time of day to avoid the hourly fluctuations in weight.

Weigh yourself without clothes, even if it does mean doing something about the draughts. And for God's sake draw the curtains. You don't want the window cleaner to have a nasty accident.

Stand evenly on the scales with both feet. No rocking backwards and forwards and taking the best offer. And no trying one foot at a time and adding up the totals.

Keep a note of your weight. Write it down while the evidence is still in front of you — before faulty memory or a guilty conscience do things to it.

If your weight's up — do something. Go a bit easier on the Red and Amber foods. No use waiting another week, by which time you could have twice as much to shift.

* * *

Now for a real shock: the weight-for-height charts.

There are variations in weight between individuals of the same height. Men weigh more than women height-for-height. And the size of your frame can affect the issue: bigger-boned people weigh more.

Many people justify their poundage by claiming to be not overweight, but under-tall. Or add a couple of inches to their height. 'About five-six, I'd say,' chirps the little butterball who would only make five-six on stilts.

Others blame it all on the bones. Either there's a high incidence of lead in the average skeleton, or a lot of fatties are direct descendants of Neanderthal Man.

Anyway, try these for size. Check your height without shoes and your weight without clothes. Where the lines cross on the chart — that's you. And remember — no cheating.

Seven-foot-two,
Eyes of blue.
She's a little fibber, too.
Has anybody seen my gal . . .?

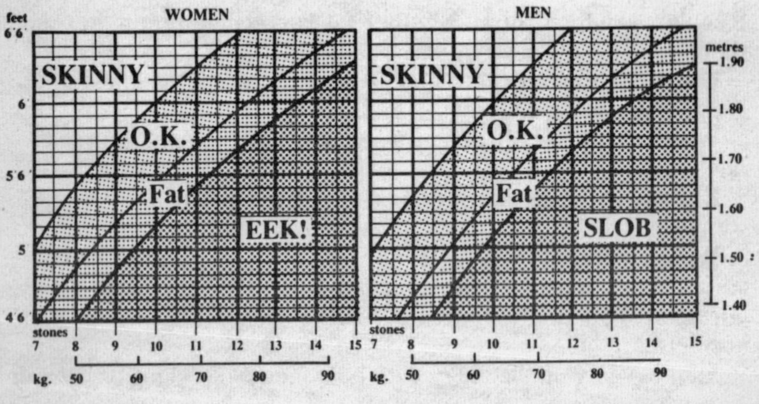

CHAPTER FOUR

All in the Mind

Every day you're being got at. Subverted. Brainwashed.

Every day millions of pounds, dollars, francs, Deutschmarks, guilders, liras and pesos — not to mention yen, dirhams and the occasional zloty — are spent in persuading you to eat more than is good for you.

There's hardly a billboard hoarding which doesn't proclaim the impossibility of living without somebody's cream-packed puffs, fat-drenched doughnuts or cholesterol-crammed crisps.

There's hardly a television commercial break without an ad for some kind of convenience food, chocolate bar, dessert topping, fish finger, parson's nose, silk purse or sow's ear.

There's hardly a newspaper or magazine which isn't packed with ads for eatables, and which doesn't carry a cookery page of marketing-board-inspired recipes at a discreet distance from the slimming page.

Most of the ads are aimed at women. And, according to a British woman lecturer in communications, they're not just tempting — they're positively rude.

'Food pornography', was how she described the glossy exhortations to stuff yourself. (See? Freudian slips already.)

The ads arouse illicit desires, she said, much as sex pornography does in men. Illicit, because although the food is being presented as the one legitimate sensual pleasure for women, they are being told simultaneously by other bodies that they shouldn't eat so much.

The pornography label pleased doctors and dieticians, but upset the advertising men, who accused her of everything from woman-hating — and man-hating, just to make sure — to insanity.

Is it pornography? Is food rude? Are calories corrupting? Is sugar the start of the sensual slide down the slippery slope? (I'd put your teeth in before you try to say that again.)

Certainly it's not hard porn. Nobody's likely to be sucked into the depths of depravity by an ad for a cream bun. But the definition of pornography is 'literature or art calculated solely to supply sexual excitement'. (Think you need your teeth for that one as well.) And the aim of the food industry ad men is to supply gastric excitement.

Consider the problems the poor lads face. No excitement means no sales. No sales, no accounts. No accounts, heads roll. Heads roll, no salaries or expenses (rolling heads gather no gross). And even ad men have to eat.

Illicit desires? What a thing to suggest. But a British dairy industry campaign for cream carried the slogan: 'Food is Naughty but Nice'.

Clever one, that. Try 'Nice but Naughty' and spot the difference.

A television campaign for some doubtless delicious but obviously fattening confection depicted suburban housewives drawing their curtains at morning coffee time to retire for a secret and solitary ritual in their darkened dining rooms.

The ritual was simply the scoffing of the confection. Not the turn-on of the century. But after the scoffing, the hausfraus were swept off their feet by macho male stereotypes — Arabs and cowboys and such, not normally thick on the ground in suburbia — who burst in through the French windows and carried them off for an unspecified purpose.

There's hardly a television ad for Turkish delight without the statutory sheikh. All flowing robes, flashing eyes and flaring nostrils. Nor one for chocolates which doesn't feature some anonymous and athletic twit risking his life to deliver a box of soft centres. After which the athletic twit leaps out of the boudoir — before the lady's even arrived — back into the night. Perhaps to meet the statutory sheikh, who by now has gone off ladies who do nothing but eat Turkish delight.

Illicit desires? Never.

It's surprising that the video porn industry hasn't cottoned on yet to the possibilities of Rude Food:

Naked Noodles!!!

Beef in the Raw!!!

Gay Cream Puffs!!!

Tristan and Isolde?
Abelard and Heloise?
Bogart and Bacall?
You've seen nothing yet!
Watch the sexiest twosome
of all time — Ham and Eggs!!!

See Spotted Dick get the
Maids of Honour in the
Pudding Club!!!

And don't miss the
Gang Bang to End
All Gang Bangs. Eggs,
Bacon, Sausages, Tomatoes,
Beans, Black Pudding and
Fried Bread — in the same pan!!!

* * *

Seriously, now — come on, pull yourself together — what can you do about the brainwashing?

You can make it easier by not looking at the ads in the first place, though it's not as easy as it sounds. They lie in wait, over the next magazine page, in the next television commercial, on the nearest hoarding. But there's nothing to stop you going for a brisk walk, closing your eyes, or sticking a paper bag over your head. Don't close your eyes or stick a paper bag over your head if you're going for a brisk walk. You might bump into the hoarding. (Should have mentioned that earlier, Parker you fool.)

The best technique is to brainwash back. Fight fire with fire. Analyse and dismiss the subversive images planted in your mind.

De-briefing, it's called in military and espionage circles. Which has led to a lot of low jokes about the undercover girl agent who was so dim that she thought de-briefing meant dropping your knickers.

(Forget it. This is serious.)

Start by looking at the contents of your fridge. All those shrink-wrapped foods. None of them came by those tempting colours naturally. If processed foods were sold without artificial colouring, they'd look like something the cat threw up. Surveys have shown definite consumer resistance to anything the cat throws up, so it's your fault. You want colour, you get colour.

The tempting spreads laid out in the magazine ads didn't look nearly so tempting in the studios. Studios are hot, and good shots take time. Ice cream melts in minutes. Other stuff congeals, goes soggy, crusts over. And even if the colours are strong enough to hold up under the arc lights, they may still not register properly on film.

Many of the dishes that look so good on glossy paper or on the television screen are not the real dishes at all. Meat is painted, varnished, injected, sprayed. Custard is probably paint. The glistening white ice cream may be yellow plaster, because the real stuff melts and the white doesn't register on film as white. The appetising steam, rising as the tureen lid is lifted, is being pumped into the dish. And it's probably not steam, but vapourising liquid oxygen or some such.

Bubbles. Nothing like bubbles for giving life to something soggy. Those bubbles in the pan as it starts to simmer. You love 'em. So the art director gives you bubbles. And he blows 'em.

All those tiny bubbles shooting up in a twinkling procession through that ice-cold drink — they're coming from an aquarium pump or a hypodermic syringe. The real drink would have gone flat as a fluke after five minutes under the arc lights.

Do you still fancy the dishes shown in the ads? Try them. Ask an advertising agency if you can eat what's on the table after they've finished shooting. See how much you can eat without breaking a tooth, throwing up or poisoning yourself.

The meals in the ads are even more attractive because they look so easy. But remember you're looking at the finished product, and you've had none of the hassle of cooking it. No sweat, lank hair, burned fingers, fat on the floor, scalded cat running yowling around the house and early dinner guests already ringing the bell.

Perhaps it's the people in the ads you envy. Those lissom, beautiful young people lounging about on tropical beaches, doing daring things on surfboards. And in between times stuffing themselves with chocolate bars, nougat bars, nutty bars, fruity bars, coconut bars. Unlikely ever to run short of chocolate-nougat-nutty-fruity-coconut bars because just behind the beach there's a cave full of them. Mysteriously never melting in the tropical heat.

Remember that the beautiful people are only pretending. They were chosen for physiques which got that way by strict refusal to touch any such bars with a ten-foot pole. If they were to eat all those calories lying around, they'd soon be waddling across the golden sands, bursting out of their briefs, sinking the heaviest-duty surfboard, and finishing their daring dives from the rocks with the most god-awful bellyflops.

Many ads put food and drink into glamorous settings. Soft lights, sweet music, attentive waiters. And slim, glamorous, jetset diners, gazing at each other over the pud with looks suggesting something even more romantic for afters.

Anybody eating and drinking regularly like that would soon be twice the size, flat broke, and in no fit state for romantic afters.

The more downmarket commercials for beer imply that it's manly to knock back all that booze. The characters are virile, no-nonsense lads supping away before going back to the building site or football field, all having a jolly good time in congenial company and being eyed smoulderingly by the ladies present. So you don't drink Frothingslosh, eh? What are you — some kind of fairy?

Unlike the genuine pub scenes, nobody's throwing up, nobody's being thrown out, nobody's in a fight, nobody's being breathalysed, nobody's being arrested. There's never an overweight drunk slumping across the bar and slurring out an order for one for the road. Nobody's going back to the building site and falling straight off the scaffolding. And nobody's getting back to his loved one with an attack of brewer's droop that makes a positive response to smouldering glances highly unlikely.

Many ads for convenience foods play on the guilt feelings or wish-fulfilment of the harassed mother. All you have to do is add hot water to the packet of instant Sludgegulp and you've a four-course meal in seconds.

Aren't you a clever old thing? Don't the kids think you're wonderful? And hasn't it put the gleam back in dad's eye? (Answers: No you're not. No they don't. And no it hasn't.)

Families drool over such stuff only on screen. What happens at home is that the kids go, 'Yuk! Not this old rubbish again!' And dad stomps off to the pub. Pausing only to kick the cat, which has already been sick on the leftovers.

* * *

Hard on the heels of the food and booze ads come the ads for bras, girdles, corsets. The easy options. Instant solutions.

So you're a little buxom, eh, Modom? A well-developed girl, are we? Have no fear — our new Floppercopper range will take care of all that. You'll look sylph-like in no time.

And on the screen appears a girl with a figure bordering on the anorexic, wearing a bondage kit that could put a wasp waist on a hippo. You, too, can have an hourglass figure. (Pity that in your case all the sand has slipped to the bottom.)

Bras? Try our Rawhide range. (*Rawhide*: Rounds 'em up and

heads 'em out.) Or the new Atomic range. (*Atomic*: Makes molehills out of mountains.) And if all else fails, try the Dictator range. (*Dictator*: Suppresses the masses.)

The reason the model looks so good in the bra is that she doesn't need it. If she did, she wouldn't be a model. What company's going to show on screen a woman big enough actually to need one of their foundation garments? Frighten anybody to death. It's not just foundations the companies are selling — it's hope.

Remember, too, that the surplus fat is not compressed by the foundation garments: if it's pushed in at one place, it's got to emerge somewhere else. In theory it's possible to control your figure by wearing the lot — support tights, pantie-girdle, navel-deep bra — and find yourself with a 44-inch head.

* * *

There are a lot of dodges you can use to take your mind off food, or even to put you off it altogether.

If you fancy a chocolate cream, for instance, imagine yourself eating it. Then imagine yourself eating another. And another. Until you're gorged with the stuff and never want to see another chocolate cream as long as you live. Then go and have a piece of crispbread to take the taste away.

A technique recommended by many doctors is for the overweight person to write down everything he or she eats during a week. Everything — and to write it down at the time of eating, so nothing gets forgotten.

The difference between what people eat and what they *think* they eat is often staggering, and enough to convince them they're overdoing things.

Sneaking down for midnight nibbles? Make it difficult. Let the tarantulas out in the kitchen before you go upstairs. Sprinkle tacks around the bed. Booby-trap the stairs. Seriously, why not lock the kitchen door and give the key to your partner to hide? And it's not going too far to fit a burglar alarm to the kitchen door: you wouldn't be able to sneak down to the fridge without waking the whole house up.

Collect revolting jokes about food and read them whenever you feel a craving coming on. Such as:

A tramp knocked at the door of the big house. When the lady of the house answered he cried piteously: 'Please help me, missus. I'm starving. All I've left to eat is this old piece of horse manure.'

'Oh, you poor man,' exclaimed the lady. 'You must be desperate. Go round the back to the stables and get yourself a fresh piece.'

Or:

The commanding officer of a Foreign Legion detachment addressed his men on a forced march.

'Men,' he said, 'we're doing well. We've only 500 miles to go to reach the next fort. Unfortunately, supplies are running a little low and I have some bad news and some good news.

'The bad news is that we've nothing to eat but camel dung.

'The good news is that there's plenty of it.'

Or:

Two sewer men were wading through the most evil-smelling filth when one dropped his handkerchief. He fished around in the foul mess until he found it.

'What did you do that for, Jim?' asked his mate. 'It wasn't worth getting yourself covered in that stuff just for a handkerchief.'

'It wasn't just a handkerchief,' said Jim. 'My sandwiches were in it.'

* * *

If you run out of jokes, you can always ponder on this next lot: some recent — and real — aids to keeping away from fattening food.

Slimming with Style

A chain of gourmet restaurants has started up in America, and is doing very well with restaurant names like *The Trimerie, Thin World, The Slender Touch* and *Skinny Haven*.

Nothing on the menu is fattening. No salt or cooking oil is used. Veal takes the place of beef. To ensure that customers know exactly what they're getting, the precise contents of the meal, plus calorie counts, are given on the menu.

Some less respectable diet restaurants are not so careful, and serve portions which are bigger than those listed on the menu. County inspectors, who normally crack down hard on restaurants with misleading menus, are holding their fire. Who's going to take a restaurateur to court for serving *more* than he promised?

Slimming by the Clock

A French professor recommended clock-watching as a slimming technique. Eat all your meals, he said, between the time you get up and three o'clock in the afternoon. The idea is that calories taken then are burned up more quickly than those taken later in the day.

The human body, said the professor, is at its lowest ebb at seven a.m., then gradually winds up to peak efficiency at three p.m.

This could be combined with Slimming by Sex. Some British

scientists worked out that the best time for making love was from four in the morning until 12 noon. The two activities needn't necessarily clash, provided the priorities are sorted out. Leading straight into the punchline of the ancient German joke: 'Dot vos goot. Now ve can eat.'

Nasty Noshing

An event calculated to take away all but the most ravenous appetite is the race in Oregon, USA, to see which customer of the Cooler Tavern can eat a can of dog food the fastest. Contestants have to finish the race — for a prize of £300 — by raising their heads and going, 'Arf, Arf!' It is not reported how many raise their heads, go 'Bleargh!' and throw up.

Another spectacle guaranteed to put you right off your grub is that of World Champion Nasty Nosher, Mr Allan Newbold, eating his way to the top. He holds the world record of 1 min. 5 secs. for eating 2½lb of nasty nosh: Liver, sheep's eyes, pigs' brains (all raw), accompanied by rice pudding, strawberry jam, lemon curd, treacle, raw eggs and dog food.

At the time of writing, he was planning to leave his native Barnsley, Yorkshire, for California to eat a 28lb bicycle, aiming to get the consumption time down from a fortnight to nine days.

How do you eat a 28lb bicycle? You mince it and mix it with more palatable food. Obvious when you think about it.

And what happens to the bicycle when it's been eaten? The polite answer is that it's recycled. Obvious when you think about it . . .

Dulldog Bummond and the Red Barrel

Of all the British fighter aces of World War One, none was more dashing and daring than jolly old Dulldog Bummond.

Of all the German fighter aces, none was more feared and hated than the villainous Baron von Bredhofen, the dreaded Red Barrel.

Dulldog Bummond was not only the most famous British fighter ace, but also the fattest: 22 stone of the Flower of British Manhood.

Baron von Bredhofen was not only the most notorious German fighter ace. He, too, was the fattest and, by a strange coincidence, also 22 stone. Of solid Teutonic lard.*

These two captains of the skies had a personal feud, which started during their very first encounter.

As the two planes roared towards each other, von Bredhofen realised the identity of his opponent. He leaned out of the cockpit of his Schmokkewulf 190 and jeered:

'Guten Morgen — Fatface!'

'I say,' thought Dulldog. 'This chappie's not playing the game. Still, whatever it is, two can play at it.'

And he leaned from the cockpit of his Slopwith Dromedary and shouted back:

'Piggy Features!'

This annoyed the Baron, who did a quick Immelmann turn and zoomed in close with:

'Hottopitamus!'

His English was not perfect, but Dulldog grasped his meaning.

Easing back the stick for a tight loop, he roared down on the German, shouting:

'Wobblychops!'

The German, who had not been to such a good school as Dulldog, replied with:

'Elephant Arse!'

Dulldog countered this vile insinuation with:

'Fat Nanny's Bottom — with knobs on!'

So the battle continued. The two little planes looped and rolled

*By the *Boys' Own Paper* rules, the British are always dashing, daring, jolly, famous and the Flower of Manhood. The Germans are feared, hated, villainous, notorious and composed entirely of lard. German readers, please transpose.

and dived and banked and turned in the clear blue skies over France to the sound of:

'Barrel Belly!'

'Listen who's talking — Droopy Drawers!'

'Bulgy Bum!'

'Pot calling kettle! Bunter Bottom!'

'Rumble Guts!'

'Georgie Porgie, Pudden and Pie!'

* * *

For almost four years this went on. The two were so busy shouting insults at each other that they never got around to firing their guns. Eventually, word reached the respective High Commands, and both Dulldog and von Bredhofen were told: 'Next time, it must be for real!'

. . . So here they were, closing in for their last, fatal encounter, with no quarter asked or given.

The battle in the air was over in minutes. Both pilots had got even fatter in the intervening time, and both found that they could not reach the gun buttons. In trying to get to his, Dulldog jammed the joystick so that the plane looped sharply out of control. The loop finished right behind von Bredhofen and the two planes collided.

Both planes, however, survived intact enough to make forced landings. The two pilots heaved and grunted their way out of the tiny cockpits and stood facing each other. The Lords of the Sky. Ironically forced to finish their last encounter on the ground.

'Vot vill it be?' asked von Bredhofen. 'Pistols? Sabres?'

'Hardly, old chap,' said Dulldog. 'I don't know about you, but I haven't brought a thing with me. It'll have to be Belly Bumpers.'

'Ach, you English!' exclaimed von B. 'Schoolboys to der last. Still, I suppose der Belly Boombers it must be.'

The two stripped off their flying suits and stood, face to face and belly to belly, for the fight to the death.

The rules of Belly Bumpers are simple. One bumps the opponent's belly with one's own, and vice versa, until one of the combatants either submits or collapses. It is an old and traditional English game, very popular with portly, middle-aged, ex-public schoolboys round about closing time.

It was familiar to von Bredhofen also, because a form of it was practised in Germany among the poorer members of university duelling fraternities: anyone who broke his sabre and could not afford to replace it was relegated to the *Bellybümperzimmer* until such time as he was in funds again.

'You first, old man,' said Dulldog.
'Ach, der chivalrous British,' said von Bredhofen. And opened with a vicious Heidelburg Humper.
Winded, Dulldog staggered back, but recovered in time to check von Bredhofen's advance with a neat Eton Endover and followed this up with a powerful Salisbury Sidewinder.
'Gott in Himmel!' gasped von Bredhofen as he countered with a Guttenberg Gonger. 'You learned your game well, my friend!'
For hours, back and forth, the battle raged. Two such well matched opponents as this had never been seen before, either in the history of aviation or of Belly Bumpers.

The end was sudden. The two were advancing towards each other at a staggering trot, Dulldog intent on a Harrow Haymaker, and von Bredhofen on a Düsseldorf Deathdealer, when von Bredhofen tripped on the churned-up turf.
The two met head on. Almost 50 stone in a bone-crushing collision.
As they lay there, feet to feet, a lone British plane flew overhead. The pilot leaned out with a megaphone.
'I say! You two down there! Good news — it's an Armistice!'
But the news fell on deaf and crumpled ears. Never again would the two titans meet in mortal combat. Or any other kind of combat.
Both had lived up to the fliers' motto:

Per
Ardua
Ad
Enough

CHAPTER FIVE

When It's Time to Get 'Em Off

Excess weight often creeps up slowly, and with many people it can be years before they will admit to being even a teensy-weensy bit on the bigsy-wigsy side.

While the pounds are piling on, the subconscious mind is busy rejecting evidence such as height-for-weight charts which imply that you are eight feet tall. Other early warning signs — pinging buttons, collapsing chairs, garrotting collars — are all put down to the fact that they don't make 'em like they used to. A tendency to sluggishness, breathlessness and accidents is easily explained by the fact that misfortunes come in threes.

Because the process is often gradual, the subconscious has time to adjust to the changing shape. The adjustment is mainly a matter of absorbing the information and instantly rejecting or suppressing it. The image of oneself remains unchanged: you slim, lovely little thing, you.

There does come a time, however, when the signs are unmistakable. When they are no longer minor inconveniences but major embarrassments, discomforts or catastrophes. A few of the more common ones are given in the check lists which follow.

If one, some or — God forbid — all are happening to you, then it's time to get 'em off. The pounds that is. Until you do, nobody's likely to ask you to discard anything else.

Women

You are overweight when:

Shortsighted people stuff envelopes in your mouth every time you stand on the corner in a red dress, or try to board you in mistake for a Number 38 bus.

Your living bra joins the Euthanasia Society.

Your bras, which used to be made by Cammell Laird, are now put out to tender in South Korea.

When you reach for your girdle in the morning, it dives for the window and screams for help.

Your 18-hour girdle demands a substitute at half time.

When you ask for support tights, the assistant says, 'Certainly madam — radial or cross-ply.'

You ask what kind of support the assistant recommends and she suggests a flying buttress.
Your lorry driver lover steals your garter — to replace a broken fan belt on his juggernaut.
Little boys chase you down the street shouting, 'Hey Missis! There's a mugger in your knickers!'
Girls on the beach ask if they can get changed behind you.
You try to buy an off-the-peg dress in the Large Ladies department and are re-directed to Camping Equipment.
Camping Equipment think you might find what you're looking for next door at the Circus Surplus sale.
Whenever your husband gets that certain gleam in his eye, he comes to bed in mountaineering gear. It's not that you mind so much as his planting a flag on the top. But did he *really* need those oxygen cylinders?

Men

You are overweight when:

You stand at the bar and can't reach your drink.
The cricket captain asks you to stand behind the wicket in your best whites. Just till the sight screen is repaired.
You turn out in goal for the football team and the opposition demands a 50 per cent increase in the distance between the posts.
You are allowed on the local bowling green only on condition that you wear snowshoes.
Your record pole vault attempt fails because the pole disappears. The award of a pole depth record is small consolation.
You try to answer a Call of Nature and find you need fire tongs to do it.
You ask for a pair of Y-fronts and the assistant tactfully suggests that you might be happier with W-fronts. Or suggests you try the XYZ range.
Your team wins the annual tug-o'war competition against the local champions. And only you have turned up.
You put the golf ball where you can see it, and find you can't hit it.
You put the golf ball where you can hit it, and find you can't see it.

Both

You are overweight when:

You need four seats at the cinema instead of the usual two.
You stand on a speak-your-weight machine and it shouts, 'Gerroff!' or 'One at a time, *please*!'

You walk down a street and all the weighing machines jump back inside the chemists' shops.
You can't make love in the back of a car. Because you can't get in the back of a car.
You step on the platform of a moving bus and the bus keeps moving. The platform is in the road, under your great fat foot.
You say to the cheeky little boy on the bus, 'Why don't you stand up and let one of those five people sit down?' And he replies, 'Why don't *you* stand up and let 'em all sit down?'
You step into the shower and your feet don't get wet.
You can't get into the shower.
The next door neighbour puts an *Ancient Lights* notice at the spot where you lean over the fence for a chat.
You join a charity team to attempt the greatest-number-of-people-in-a-telephone-box record. And your team scores one.
You are asked to leave a health food shop on the grounds that it's bad for business.
The drama society casts you for the crowd scene. On your own.
You go to a local fatstock show and come out with a rosette stuck between your eyes.
You bend down at the races and a shortsighted stable boy slaps a saddle on your back and pushes a pep pill down your throat.
The road gang foreman explains that the steamroller has run out of steam, and would you mind tap dancing on the hole they have just filled in?
Every time you fall down, you rock yourself to sleep trying to get up.
You are taller lying down than standing up.

On holiday, you walk down to the beach for a bathe and the tide goes out.
You dive off the pier and tidal waves wreck 50 miles of coastline.
You need a snorkel for water ski-ing.
You go for a dip and the coastguard is alerted to look out for a drifting marker buoy.
You lie on the beach and a whale rescue squad from Greenpeace rolls you down to the sea.
On a visit to the zoo, a myopic mahout sticks a big hook behind your ear and shouts, 'Jildi, O lovely Nellie!'
You approach the elephant ride and the elephant gives a passionate mating call. Or rushes off to find the nearest elephants' graveyard.
You yawn by the side of the hippo pool and finish up with a mouthful of peanuts.
You climb on the kneeling camel and it can't get up.
The camel does get up, but finishes the ride with the hump underneath.
The camel finishes the ride intact, but immediately drops dead. Muttering, 'Some bloody straw . . .'
The airline bills you for 100lb excess baggage. And you don't have any baggage.
You are refused admission to the Leaning Tower of Pisa on the grounds that it's done all the leaning it dare do.
You step aboard a cruise ship and the Plimsoll line disappears.
You step aboard the *Skylark* for a trip around the lighthouse and the *Skylark* disappears.

CHAPTER SIX

Shapes of Things to Come

Despite the horrifying statistics on obesity, there's little doubt that thousands of people, especially women, are slimming unnecessarily simply to keep in fashion, or out of the idea that *any* fat at all is disgusting. At its worst it has led to many cases of *anorexia nervosa* over the past decade.

Often arising out of a subconscious desire not to grow up and have to face the world, anorexia is literally starvation. It affects fertility — it can stop the menstrual cycle altogether — plays havoc with general health, and has in more than a few cases resulted in death. Anorexia is not at all nice.

There is a wider tendency amongst otherwise level-headed women of perfectly respectable size and shape to worry about their curves. They're bombarded daily through the fashion and diet pages with the message that Thin is Beautiful, and often will diet to live up to the image and fit into the slimline fashions. From the man's point of view — there's no evidence that men have changed their attitudes towards a good handful — it seems a pity.

The changed diets and lifestyles of the past 25 years seem to have had permanent effects. A survey of 4,500 women by a British anthropologist showed that, in that time, women have become more like men. They are taller, have smaller busts, thicker waists and slimmer hips.

By the year 2000, if the trend continues, it may be hard to spot the difference.

But one of these days, all the questions of size, shape and weight could be purely academic. An American gynaecologist and science fiction writer has predicted that we shall all finish up as 'small, brown creatures, no more than 5ft in height'.

We'll be incredibly healthy, long lived and 'necessarily gregarious'. That last is a bit puzzling, as by then we'll have 'large, hairless, domed heads and small, pointed, pixie-like faces with tiny, toothless mouths'. And to the casual onlooker, both males and females will look alike.

Where the motivation for gregariousness will come from when we're all bald, toothless dwarfs — even allowing for the uniform 'pleasing, tawny colour' — is hard to see. Even the sex urge may be a bit dampened by having nobody to indulge it with except a look-alike.

Singles Nights could be punctuated with Max Miller-type cries of, 'Thank you, lady . . . Thank you, lady . . . Sorry, Fred! Thank you, lady . . .'

The one consolation is that the change will probably take hundreds of thousands of years. By then we'll be past caring.

* * *

An American biologist (why does it *always* have to be Americans?) sees the days of smaller people arriving much earlier. Problems of overcrowding and food shortages could be solved, he says, by shrinking the human race.

For a generation or two, only small people would be allowed to breed. As the big people died off, the world would become populated by midgets between two and three feet tall.

'Think of the advantages,' he says. 'Smaller appetites, a fairer distribution of food, plummeting transport costs as more people fit into cars and planes — and no housing shortages.'

But what about the disadvantages? Cars and planes immobile because nobody's feet could reach the pedals. Being locked out of the house at night because you couldn't reach the keyhole. And the occasional five-foot, seven-stone throwback walking up the beach and kicking sand in your face.

CHAPTER SEVEN

No Cheating

Some people cheat about their weight right from the start by refusing even to admit that they are fat. Can you credit it? You, whose shape has barely altered at all over the years, and whose weight has remained constant — give or take a pound or two — you are keeping a sharp eye open for the first signs of incipient obesity.

Of course you wouldn't cheat. What's the point? Where's the sense? But you might be one of the 97.5 fat people who cheat unconsciously. (The other 2.5 per cent cheat consciously.)

The breathlessness caused by walking a quarter of a mile with a bag of shopping is not caused by any extra poundage of yours. It's the weight of the packet of crispbread and half-dozen ping pong balls in the shopping bag.

What is aggravating the whole thing is the fact that that particular stretch of road has tilted to an angle of 33 degrees to the horizontal over the past 12 months, making the whole journey an uphill struggle. Must write to the council about the subsidence.

The total collapse when you finally leapt on that bus after a marathon 25-yard dash. The pounding heart, the heaving chest, the death-rattle in the throat. They were not caused by your carrying too much weight to run for buses. You've never felt fitter in your life.

No, the bus accelerated, that's all. It must have been doing forty by the time you leapt aboard. You could have told the conductor that you had just broken the world speed record over the distance from a standing start, not to say given him a piece of your mind, if you hadn't turned purple and crumpled at his feet.

You, sir. You seem to be sweating a lot these days. A quick prod at the flowerbed with the garden fork and you're dripping. Even changing your mind brings out the beads on the old forehead.

Not that this is anything to worry about. The melting of polar ice caps is changing the world's climate. Eventually you will get used to it. The climate in what are now temperate areas will be verging on the tropical in another 10,000 years or so. By which time your body mechanism will have adjusted. By which time, anyway, because all the polar ice will have melted, you will be up to your neck in water.

Your suit. They don't make 'em like they used to. Bit snug here and there? Jacket straining a little across the middle button? You've tried a link button and that's just pinged off as well? They can't get the cloth these days. That Taiwan rubbish shrinks as soon as you look at it. Tight around the chest, too? Must be all those credit cards in your wallet. One of the penalties of prosperity.

Trousers. Perhaps slipping under the overhang of abdominal muscle caused by all that weight-training you did as a youth. Giving your legs this year's fashionable concertina look and allowing your shirt to billow out romantically like the mainsail of the *Hispaniola*. Arrr, Jim lad! A foine figure ye're cuttin', to be sure!

Or perhaps the trousers are not slipping under. They're riding over. Assisted by the braces you started wearing when the belt shrank. A bit snug under the chin these days.

A bit snugger, too, at the top of the inside leg. Giving you frostbite around the ankles on account of the calf-length bottoms. Giving you that stiff-legged walk which worked wonders for the Third Reich for a while. Giving you a bearing so erect that you're leaning backwards 15 degrees from the vertical. Bringing tears to your eyes on account of the extra-snug sawing action in the area where the tailor sticks the cold metal end of his tape measure. Making you avoid climbing stairs for fear of being cut to the quick. And leaving only one answer when the tailor asks, 'How do you dress?'

Painfully.

You're having trouble, too, madam. Your dress. Shrinks every time you put it in the wash. And goes further out of shape.

The hem rides up at the front, giving the curious illusion of fat and dimpled knees. Funny how it can do that to a pair of trim little kneecaps which were once the magnet for a hundred hands in the backs of taxis.

Whenever you bend down, the hem rides up at the back. Creating another curious illusion which causes ill-mannered little lads to shout, 'Thar she blows!'

The bodice. Upon which buttons will not stay longer than the first deep breath. That embarrassing encounter with the milkman when you laughed at his joke and machine-gunned him with mother-of-pearl.

You wouldn't care, but it's not only dresses that are shoddy these days. Your roll-on. Which suddenly shrank so much it refused to roll. Leaving you no alternative but to use the shoehorn. You managed it all right, painful though it was. But then had to spend another two hours retrieving the shoehorn.

That bra. The trouble you have with it. Bad enough having to mend the straps and replace the hooks and eyes every other day. But you can't even trust it to hold anything in any more.

The shame and mortification of the dinner at the Savoy. When you took a deep breath to make room for the Coq au Vin. And your right boob did a somersault. Landing on the Coq and splashing everyone with Vin.

It was nice of that young waiter to grasp the situation so quickly. Drawing on his white gloves to replace the errant appendage. Delicately removing bits of parson's nose and wiping it down with a clean napkin before he did so.

Terrible, wasn't it, that the head waiter was so furious?

'At the Savoy,' he hissed, glaring down at the cowering young *commis*, 'we use a silver soup ladle. Warmed.'

The poor boy was so embarrassed. As he explained to his friends later, 'I felt a right tit.'

Bad enough when a bra starts letting you down. But look what's happening to your knickers. Elastic breaking so often that a walk down to the shops sounds like *High Noon* on an understrung guitar. Gussets giving way as soon as you step outside the door.

There's no doubt about it. The bottom has dropped out of the knicker market.

* * *

Perhaps you have been looking at yourself lately in a cold and objective light, and decided that you should lose the odd ounce or two. Nothing drastic. Just a whisker off the wobbly bits and a soupçon off the saggy ones. And you've embarked on a strict diet.

Dieting takes willpower. Of which, luckily, you have a superabundance. And which ensures that you play it strictly by the book.

You have cut out bread and potatoes for a start. Making do with toast and chips.

You stick strictly to the prescribed mealtime diet. For breakfast, lunch, dinner and supper, not a morsel passes your lips that is not on the diet sheet.

Not that the diet is doing you a bit of good, the way the wobbly bits are getting wobblier and the saggy bits getting saggier. Apart from anything else, the strict mealtime regime makes you feel so weak and hungry all the time. If it were not for the odd cup of tea and doughnut, packet of crisps, ham roll, Danish pastry, cream bun, biscuits and the slice of lardy cake that you have at odd moments, you don't know how you'd get through the day.

Funny, those saggy and wobbly bits. It's not as if you don't get plenty of exercise.

You, sir, read somewhere that walking is the best all-round exercise. So every evening now you walk the hundred yards down to the pub instead of getting the car out. Not that it doesn't have its compensations. You can sink the extra couple or three pints now without having to worry about meeting the Law on the way back.

And you do your press-ups every morning. Ten of them. Well, not quite ten. There isn't time for all those first thing, what with shaving and all. Five. All right, then. Two. They perhaps would be more effective if your stomach left the floor, but you read somewhere that too much sudden strain on the back can be dangerous. You're not cheating at all: just taking sensible precautions.

You, madam, get plenty of exercise with all that housework. And you do the breakfast television exercises with Lucy Lastic and tune in on the radio to Seamus O'Leprechaun's work-out. Well, you *start* with Lucy Lastic's routine, but find it a bit strenuous in the grey light of dawn, apart from never remembering where you put your leotard. (In the summer, the kids *will* keep borrowing it for a tent.)

And Seamus O'Leprechaun will insist on saying Irish naughties such as, 'Give me your body . . . It's your thoighs Oi'm afther . . .' Which gets you in such a state that you've got to lie down until the feeling wears off.

* * *

To sum up:

1. You're not fat. Just suffering from unexpected bursts of speed, heatwaves and clothes with built-in obsolescence.

2. The wobbles and saggies are purely the result of some temporary metabolic disturbance with which you have been afflicted despite strict adherence to diet and exercise routines.

3. It's not you who have changed. It's the world.

CHAPTER EIGHT

It's Like This, Doctor . . .

No cheater, you, that's for sure. And certainly not given to self-deception. Not like the fatties who turn up regularly at doctors' surgeries with weight problems they can't understand . . .

Caught Short

'It's my height, you see. I'm only five-foot-four.'

'But dammit — you're 16 stone.'

'I know. I should be seven-foot-two.'

Glandular Fever

'I can't do much about my weight. It's my glands.'

'Which ones?'

'How do I know which ones? You're the doctor.'

For the Birds

'Can't understand it. I eat like a bird.'

'Then you'll be pleased to hear the equivalent diet for a human: eat half your own weight in food every day.'

'Yummee yummee. What kind of food?'

'Worms.'

The Answer's a Lemon

'I swear by lemon juice.'

'Cuts the weight down, does it?'

'It must do. Stands to reason. At least it cuts out that horrible greasy feeling after sausages and chips.'

Baby Talk

'Of course, once you've had a baby, it's difficult to get back to normal. I've never been the same since Sidney was born.'

'Ah, yes. Sidney. How is he?'

'Very well. It's his 21st next week.'

The Family Way

'When you're cooking for the family it's impossible to resist the odd nibble.'

'How many children do you have, then?'

'Just the one. He's nearly six months. But then there's my husband coming home at all hours and wanting to be fed.'

'What's his job?'

'A lighthouse keeper.'

Occupational Hazard
'It's the job. I need all that food to get through a heavy day at work. Sometimes I shift two tons of bricks in an hour.'
'You're a hod carrier, then?'
'No. A forklift truck driver.'

Chocolate Dropsy
'Chocolates are my only vice. Then only the soft centres. And I never eat them at home; just at work.'
'And what's your job?'
'Packer.'
'Packing what?'
'Chocolates.'

Tough at the Top
'I blame all these business lunches. There's no escape. Not that I'm keen on all this foreign muck they dish up in restaurants. Too rich for me. Give me plain, honest home cooking every time.'
'Sounds much more sensible.'
'Yes. There are days when I just can't wait to get home to the wife's mixed grill.'

Water with It
'I only drink scotch. Not fattening if you take it with water.'
'How many scotches a day do you drink?'
'Ten or 12 doubles. Give or take.'
'But that's twelve or fifteen hundred calories, give or take. What does the water do?'
'Drowns 'em, I suppose.'

More Water with It
'Don't know what you're fussing about. My father ate six meals and drank 20 pints of bitter every day of his life. Until the day he died. Never did him any harm.'
'A remarkable man. How old was he when he died?'
'Thirty-two'.

Boozer's Doom
'What do I drink during the day? Not a lot. Lunchtimes, just the odd six pints of bitter, a couple of bottles of stout and perhaps a large scotch to finish off.'
'*That's* all?'
'To be truthful, sometimes I do nip out earlier in the morning for a livener.'
'I really would suggest that you cut down. It's a fair old intake for one day.'
'You're dead right, doc. I'll do that. Anything rather than cut down in the evenings.'

CAUTIONARY TALES FOR FAT PEOPLE: 2

The Sugar Plum Fairy

Once upon a time, in the meadow just beyond the Wild Wood, lived a kind fairy. Her name was Gossamer, but everybody who knew her well called her Sugar Plum.

The fairies, the elves, the gnomes, the goblins, the brownies and all the little animals of the Wild Wood, loved Gossamer very dearly for her kind heart and loving ways.

She was always ready to help anybody in trouble. A baby rabbit which had lost its way, a spider whose web had been broken, a snail which had mislaid its shell, a fieldmouse whose nest had blown down, a glow worm whose light was fading — they could always count on Fairy Gossamer to come to the rescue.

Only one thing gave Gossamer more pleasure than helping somebody, and that was eating a plump, glistening sugar plum.

The fairies, the elves, the gnomes, the goblins, the brownies and all the little animals of the Wild Wood, knew about this. So every time Gossamer did a good deed — and there were many and more every day — she was rewarded with a sugar plum or two.

And so she got her name. In time, Gossamer was forgotten. She had become The Sugar Plum Fairy.

As the weeks and the months went by, she had to work very hard to do her good deeds. Because every day she grew a little more. Sideways.

Her tiny wings had to beat harder and faster every time she went out to help somebody. So hard and fast did they have to beat that before long they became quite frayed at the edges.

Every night she was busy, too, sewing up her cobweb gown where the seams had burst. She was so tired after all this that she would have an extra sugar plum for a treat before she went to bed.

One day she went to the rescue of Grumbly Goblin, an ugly and cantankerous creature, who by rights should not have been out in daylight. The morning mist had deceived him, however. He was still wandering the Wild Wood when the sun came up and cleared the mist away, leaving him blinded by the light.

Sugar Plum heard his cries. Though her frayed wings would hardly carry her, she flew to the clearing where Grumbly was staggering around in circles, took him by the hand, and led him to the cave under the hill which was his home.

'Fairy Sugar Plum,' he said. 'I am but an ugly and cantankerous goblin, and too poor to afford a sugar plum with which to reward you. But I can offer you my hand in marriage. If you would do me the honour of accepting, who knows — I might even turn into a handsome fairy prince.'

'Alas, ugly and cantankerous goblin,' said Sugar Plum sweetly (thinking, 'Chance would be a fine thing. Prince Schmince.'), 'this could not be. You are too ugly and cantankerous. Besides, if I were to keep house for you all day, how would I find time to do my good deeds and earn my sugar plums?'

With a wave of her wand and a flurry of her frayed wings, she flew panting back home. She was becoming a little worried about her size. From her normal weight of two wisps of thistledown, she had grown to 1lb 3oz (this was in the old days of sensible weights and measures). And 1lb 3oz is heavy for a fairy.

Now, the fairies, the elves, the gnomes, the goblins, the brownies and all the little animals of the Wild Wood, heard about Sugar Plum's latest good deed, and how Grumbly Goblin had been too poor to reward her. So the next night, by the light of the full moon, they all gathered together in the Fairy Dell.

Each had brought a sugar plum. This, they said, would be the biggest and best present that Sugar Plum had ever had — and all for helping an ugly and cantankerous goblin.

'Sugar Plum!' they called through the trees. 'Come down to the Fairy Dell in the Wild Wood and see what a surprise awaits you!'

Pausing only to sew up the seams in her dress, which had split again with the effort of flying back home, Sugar Plum took off on her poor, frayed wings and flew to the Fairy Dell. There, the fairies, the elves, the gnomes, the goblins, the brownies and all the little animals of the Wild Wood, were gathered around the Magic Toadstool, the Throne of Honour reserved for special guests.

'The Magic Toadstool!' they all cried. 'Land on the Magic Toadstool!'

Sugar Plum did this, alighting shyly on the edge and folding her poor, frayed wings.

The Magic Toadstool was not built for 1lb 3oz fairies. It collapsed. Sugar Plum fell off and broke her neck.

'Serve her right,' muttered ugly and cantankerous Grumbly Goblin from the back of the crowd. 'Interfering old cow.'

CHAPTER NINE

How to Cheat

Now that you're established as a sober, upright and honest citizen whom nobody would suspect of cheating, you're ready to start.

It could be not so much that you're big, but that the things around you are small. You may look a bit silly struggling in and out of that mini-car, for a start. So try something bigger. A Mercedes. A Rolls. A Cadillac. A ten-ton truck.

It'll cost money? Of course it'll cost money. Leave you a lot less to stuff your face with.

And think of the prestige. You'll be beyond sordid thoughts of money when the neighbours start admiring your new form of transport.

('Who does he think he is? Show-off. And *her*. She never came by that car through honest toil.')

Ignore them. Or annoy them further by pinching the line from the late and overweight multi-millionaire, Nubar Gulbenkian. As he once said about his new custom-built and impossibly expensive car: 'It'll turn on a sixpence. Whatever that is.'

The house, too. You'll have to do something about that semi. You'd look far less conspicuous standing outside one of the stately homes. By Blenheim Palace, for instance, you'd look positively weeny.

Have a word with your bank manager. He'll understand. He's probably had fantasies like that all his life, and he'll respond to your request for a loan with a cheery, 'Get out!'

Should the cash not stretch to drastic changes in your home environment, you can at least organise your social life better. Instead of arranging to meet people outside Woolworth's, arrange to meet them outside St Paul's Cathedral or the Albert Hall. In Paris, choose the Arc de Triomphe. In Rome, the Colosseum. Even Nero looked slim beside the Colosseum.

Airports are no problem. In the cavernous lounges or by the jumbo jets, everybody looks tiny. If you're meeting somebody off the boat, arrange to stand in front of the *QE2*. If later they say, 'The *QE2*? I didn't notice her,' you'll really have to do something about that weight.

Don't take anybody to a meal in a small or crowded restaurant.

Always choose a big one with plenty of spare tables. A big restaurant with plenty of spare tables is usually an indication that the food's lousy. And what could be better? Already you're getting to grips, and possibly gripes, with your eating problem.

* * *

So much for your surroundings. What can you do about your actual shape?

Women can start straight away with a new set of foundation garments. Choose them yourself: don't send anybody else, especially your husband. They've no idea, husbands.

Often they'll buy something several sizes too small. Either because they remember you as you were, or because they're trying to shame you by getting into something smaller.

One unprincipled husband beknown to the author used to call into a Soho knicker boutique every year on his wife's birthday and buy his dearly beloved a full set of Saucy Nancy sexy-type underwear. Peek-a-boo bras, G-string knickers, bootlace bikinis and negligees which would fit only an anorexic Watutsi.

But why? You may well ask. Since the lady was in no fit condition to get into anything smaller than a bell tent.

'Three reasons,' said the unprincipled husband person.

'One. It makes buying birthday presents so much easier.

'Two. She's flattered. It shows that, in my eyes, she's still the lissom young thing I married.

'Three. It makes sure that at least once a year she gets off her fat arse and goes down to Weight Watchers.'

Rotten, that, wasn't it? But at least he realised that his wife was spreading. Other husbands have no idea.

Like the man who stood blushing by the lingerie counter and said, 'I'd like a bra for my wife, please.'

'Certainly sir. What size?'

'Thirteen and three-quarters.'

'I'm afraid we don't carry any such size, sir. How do you work it out?'

'Well, my bowler hat's six and seven-eighths. And that fits one of 'em.'

* * *

Don't attempt to squeeze into either girdles or bras a size too small. They may squeeze in the bits they cover very flatteringly, but will shove out the surplus top and bottom, giving you measurements of something like 42-44-42-36-42-44-42 and a shape like a stack of burst tyres waiting for a re-tread.

Your own assessment of your width is bound to be on the optimistic side, so get the fitter or assistant to measure you.

Ignore the sharp intake of breath and headshakes of disbelief. And don't panic if you hear her muttering, 'A hundred and twenty . . .' She'll be doing it in centimetres, just to show off, and you get lots more of them to the foot.

Thick thighs? A long-legged pantie girdle is best for coping with these. If you're thick all the way down, you'd best throw in a pair of support tights, elasticated long johns or heavy duty waders.

To make sure your girdle or corset is comfortable, sit down in it. If you hear a noise like, 'Zzzzzccccchhhhh!', followed by an immense feeling of relief, it's split.

Official advice on buying a bra is: 'Take about half a dozen bras into the fitting room. And if you don't immediately find one that is perfect in every way, send for more. Don't be tempted to buy in a rush.'

Let's assume that you have been allowed to take the half dozen bras into the fitting room and that the assistant is not standing on the other side of the curtain tapping her foot impatiently. Or announcing in a loud voice: 'Hasn't Modom found one to fit *yet*? The last time we had this problem was when two midgets collapsed in the shop and we had to improvise a stretcher.'

Take no notice. Official instructions for trying on a bra are: 'Lean forward so that your breasts fall naturally into the cups. Then straighten up to fasten the back before you start to adjust the shoulder straps.'

If your breasts don't fall naturally into the cups, i.e. if they fall on the floor, you need a bigger bra. If they do fall naturally into the cups, but you can't straighten up:

(a) They're heavier than you thought.

(b) Your firm-control girdle was designed more for firmness than control.

(c) You've put your back out.

But don't panic. Get yourself sorted out and then try the next step: adjusting the shoulder straps.

The straps should not need to be tight to give you the uplift you're after. If when you straighten up you go cross-eyed or your arms drop off, you need wider straps or a differently shaped bra.

Shape is important. Too pointed and you may not be able to turn around without sweeping all the ornaments off the mantelpiece. Another shape may seem to hold the breasts perfectly, but have shoved rolls of fat under the arms or even round the back.

It's no good looking svelte from the side if you can't drop your arms below your shoulders. Nor does it add to your pneumatic charms to have a second pair of boobs on your back. The man in your life could look upon them as a bonus when he comes across them, but he's more likely to pass out.

* * *

Now for your clothes. There's one sure way for either sex to look slimmer instantly: buy a blouse/shirt, outfit/suit a couple of sizes too big. You'll have friends saying, 'My — your diet certainly *is* starting to work.' Even better: 'Sure you're all right? You're looking painfully thin. Well, not painfully but . . . know what I mean?'

Both sexes are advised *not* to wear:

Large checks, unless you want the local kids to play hopscotch all over you.

Shoes with round toes or moccasins. Even overweight Red Indians have reservations about moccasins.

Large-brimmed hats, unless you want to look like an ambulant mushroom.

Bracelets, or rings on your chubby little fingers. (Certainly none on your chubby little toes.)

Light or bright shades. These make you look bigger and nearer. You look big enough from far off: no sense in making things worse.

Nubbly tweeds. Nubbly is from the word *nub*, which means knob, protuberance, lump or small piece. So don't go around covered in knobs, protuberances, lumps or small pieces. You've got enough of your own.

Horizontal stripes. Not even a deckchair wears these.

Pockets which bulge. You're bulging well enough without.

. . . And never get photographed in profile. ('Difficult to decide on your best side, sir/madam. You don't appear to *have* a side . . .')

* * *

Women should go for small prints, small checks, muted colours, in materials which are smooth, matt-surfaced, closely woven and with a 'vertical' look about them. Go for the simple lines and try to look all of a piece from top to bottom (sorry, top to toe), using the same colour tones throughout.

Things to avoid are:

Bright floral patterns. Unless you're a keen gardener and want to win the Best Herbaceous Border Without Really Trying award.

Mini skirts. Won't look good on maxi you.

Frills. Make you look like a fairy on a Christmas tree. And the Christmas tree hasn't been grown which could take you on. Well, not for long.

Furs. If you want to see the extra bulk which fur puts on, just stick the cat under the tap or dunk the dog in the water butt. And they're positively alopecic by furry standards. It's not nice, anyway. For every bit of fluff, something much smaller and slimmer than you has bitten the dust.

Accessories. If you're big busted, don't wear obtrusive jewellery above the waist. Brooches on the bosom and dangly beads draping your superstructure may do things for your presence, but in the wrong company you may find your presence felt.

Thick, patterned or white stockings. Or bobby sox. Please, not bobby sox. You can dress mutton as lamb, but not a pair of prime hams.

Three-quarter coats. These defy all the laws of mathematics. Three quarters plus the quarter that's left add up to two and a quarter.

Trousers. Not unless you're happy with your back view in a mirror.

If your back view won't fit in the mirror, it doesn't matter how happy you are.

A bikini. Oh, for God's sake. Do everybody a favour.

* * *

Men are advised to wear single-breasted coats with longer lapels and split shoulders. What this means is an inset front and raglan back, not simply splitting the shoulders by taking a deep breath.

Choose dark colours with vertical stripes.

Single-breasted, three-button suits are very slimming, provided you don't over-cheat and buy one so snug that the middle button shoots the barman after your second pint of bitter.

Avoid double-breasted styles, even though you are double breasted.

Choose trousers with a straight-cut leg and pleats to hide the bulges. The pleats should run from top to bottom, not from side to side, no matter how much all the nice girls love a sailor.

Wear lace-up shoes, and socks that carry through the colour of the trousers. A tunnel waistband or matching belt will help stop you looking like a sack of wotsit tied up in the middle.

Shirts or jumpers should be loose fitting. Certainly avoid any kind of nipped-in or slimline look unless you enjoy the sound of splitting seams and don't mind going cross-eyed or turning purple.

* * *

The most common accessory of many people is the dog. If you want to look smaller out on your morning walks, you *must* get a big one.

It's one of Nature's psychological quirks that small people go in for big dogs, and vice versa. The skinny little man or petite girl gets dragged all over the place by an Alsation, Dobermann pinscher, Hound of the Baskervilles or a shire horse in a fun fur which turns out on closer inspection to be an old English sheepdog.

It could be that the skinny person needs an aid to personality projection, or perhaps unconsciously feels the need for protection.

As soon as someone puts on weight, he or she switches to miniature poodles, Yorkshire terriers, pekes or chihuahuas. This is not good for the owner, who immediately looks twice the size. Nor is it good for the dog, which tends to get stepped on, sat on or crushed to death in loving embraces.

So to help you look smaller, buy a bigger dog, the biggest you can find or think you can handle. A Great Dane is the biggest, but tends to look lean and athletic, so the contrast is not all that it could be.

Bulk for length, a St Bernard is probably the best bet. Besides which, you can always tap it for a drink.

Big dogs have a few drawbacks which you must be prepared to face.

1 They take up a lot of house room, so you must be prepared to move to a bigger place. If you are cheating seriously, this is probably what you intended doing anyway.

2 They eat a lot, cadge from complete strangers, steal from neighbours' dustbins and compost heaps, and generally set a bad example.

3 They like comfort and have a habit of appropriating favourite armchairs. When ordered off, if they take any notice at all, they express their objections with a snarl or low growl. When belaboured with a rolled-up newspaper, they express their objections by taking a piece out of you.

4 They tend to upset postmen, old ladies and other dog owners. Especially other dog owners, because of their habit of taking an amorous interest in their little Frou-Frou and refusing to take no for an answer. Old ladies they merely bark at and give palpitations to. Postmen they attempt to eat.

5 They need a lot of exercise. They think nothing of a six-mile romp, morning and evening. After you've tried it once, you won't think much of it either.

After a few months of this you won't need to cheat at all: you'll be a shadow of your former self. The cost of the new house, the dog food, the lawsuits brought by palpitating old ladies, half-eaten postmen and dog owners with pregnant pedigree Frou-Frous, will leave you very little with which to indulge your own appetites. You'll have less to nourish, anyway, after belabouring the dog a few times and having a few pieces taken out of you. And what's left will be dragged over hill and dale at a rate of knots in very jolly twice-daily six-mile romps. Do you the world of good.

* * *

If you want to join the cheating superstars, or if you're so far gone that you need a really *big* pet, try an elephant.

Other large pets you can discount. Though the giraffe can stand 19ft in its socks and certainly weighs more than you do, the general effect is to make you look short and dumpy. Not only that, its camouflage could easily blend with the carpet and you'd keep tripping over it.

You probably wouldn't look too bad beside a hippo or rhino. Both, however, are notoriously bad tempered. The hippo is

impossible to housetrain and, its diet being what it is, makes a mess on the carpet beside which an elephant's is positively tidy. Any attempt at housetraining by correction or chastisement is met with a typical bad-tempered hippo response such as biting your leg off.

Rhinos are extemely shortsighted, which is a cause of much of the bad temper. They can't walk more than five yards without bumping into something.

So an elephant it is. The African elephant is the biggest land animal of all, can top 11ft in height and weighs around six tons. If by the side of that you still look large, you've definitely been overdoing things.

African elephants, however, are also a bit short on temper and have an awkward habit of trampling people to death or bashing them against trees. Better to settle for the Indian elephant, which, though a bit smaller, is more docile.

Choose a she-elephant: in the mating season the bull goes bananas and may do the odd bit of trampling or bashing. Though the occurrences are not frequent, and though the elephant is always sorry afterwards, they are enough to bring in complaints from neighbours or, in severe cases of trampling or bashing, from their next of kin.

Elephant upkeep comes expensive: it can shift hundreds of pounds of food a day and needs purpose-built heated quarters, preferably outside the house. To offset that, you'll never be short of manure for your kitchen garden crops of slimming greens and other fibre-filled veg. You may rupture yourself trying to shovel it, but you can't have everything.

Exercise is not the problem it is with dogs. Elephants move at a slow, steady pace, and are quite happy to give you a lift on the way back.

They can restrict your social life, though this may not be a bad thing. They are seldom welcome in pubs, for instance. Landlords are not keen on clearing up the mess on the floor after they've gone, nor on their inroads into the free peanuts, crisps and cheese nibbles laid out on the bar.

The sight of them is no comfort to habitual drinkers, either. After years of happy acceptance of lots of little pink elephants, regular boozers will take sudden and panic-stricken objection to the sight of even a solitary full-sized grey one.

Elephants themselves are also fond of the Demon Drink, and spend many happy hours in their native jungles getting happily smashed on fermenting fruit. This is OK in the jungle, where they can stagger about to their heart's content, but a drunken elephant in the averge four-ale bar doesn't do the furniture any good. Not only that, if you're standing the drinks it doesn't do your wallet any good. Two hundred pints of draught bitter on the slate and you were only in there 20 minutes.

Other snags include the fact that you can't take the thing on the bus. Not downstairs, at least. And, drunk or sober, it refuses to travel upstairs because of its inborn fear of heights.

The biggest snag of all comes at the foot of an escalator when you are confronted by a notice saying 'All animals must be carried'. Ask anyone who has tried to carry an elephant up an escalator and he'll tell you it's not worth the effort. (It's hardly worth the effort of asking, either, as you generally need a medium to do it.)

CHAPTER TEN

Anyone for Exercise?
1: An Eight-letter Word

Exercise! Eek! Who mentioned exercise?

Calm down. Anybody would think it was a dirty word.

Meanwhile, what **about** *exercise? Is it really necessary? Does it get rid of fat?*

Accept first that the human body is perhaps the most adaptable in the animal kingdom. It can run, jump, climb, drag, lift, swim and fight. It's because it can do all of these things that we're still around: that from relatively weak and defenceless animals we evolved into expert hunters, trappers and gatherers.

Our bodies were designed to cope with almost any survival task demanded of them — and that meant being almost constantly on the move. Civilisation has caught up with us and made physical movement almost redundant. But our bodies haven't changed: they still need plenty of activity to funtion properly.

So exercise really **is** *necessary. But what does it actually do?*

It keeps your heart in regular trim for a start, and gets the old blood moving around properly to where it's needed to nourish joints and muscles, take away waste products and repair moving parts.

Regular exercise not only cuts the risk of a heart attack — it improves the chances of surviving one.

Creaky joints, aching backs and bad posture can all be helped by regular activity. Flabby muscles get their tone and strength back. Before you've lost any weight, you already begin to look better and feel better.

Stress — one of today's real threats to mind and body — is eased away by gentle, rhythmic exercise. And the healthy tiredness afterwards (*healthy* tiredness: nobody's asking you to slog till you drop) helps towards untroubled and refreshing sleep.

It's fun — or it is if you make it fun. It's an added interest to life, fills in otherwise boring patches, can even bring you new friends.

You feel good: toned up, alert but relaxed, in mind and body.

Does it get rid of fat?

Take the last three points for a start. Exercise helps to get rid of stress and boredom, helps you to sleep, makes you feel good.

What happens when you're uptight, can't sleep, are bored or

feeling down? More than likely you eat or booze for solace. Already something positive is taking the place of solace. You don't need it any more.

OK. There's less fat being taken aboard. But does exercise get rid of the stuff that's already there?

Yes. Not spectacularly at the beginning, though you do start feeling better, standing better, looking trimmer. You'd have to walk a hell of a long way to lose a pound through the direct effect of the exertion (it would take an hour's brisk walk to get rid of the calories in a quarter-pound helping of suet pudding, for instance). But it has its effects over the months, providing that your food intake doesn't increase. (Cut down on your food as well and you'll *really* see results.)

It depends on the exercises, too. An hour's brisk walking uses up about 400 calories: the same as half-an-hour's hard swimming.

The big plus is that many experts believe that regular exercise, i.e. three or more times a week, increases the body's metabolic rate — the speed at which it burns up calories. So that even when you're not out walking, jogging, cycling, swimming, or whatever — even when you're asleep — your food intake is being burned up more efficiently.

Not that it's any excuse for a peanut butter sandwich before you go to bed.

* * *

Health experts recommend exercises which involve movement of the larger muscles, particularly those of the legs. They are termed *dynamic* exercises, as opposed to *static*. Static exercises include isometrics and certain body-building exercises which involve muscle contraction against resistance without any significant movement of the limbs. Static exercises, though fine for building muscle, can bring on sudden rises in blood pressure which tend not to do the middle-aged or overweight much good.

Dynamic exercises can start with something as basic as walking or climbing stairs, and go on to more athletic pursuits such as cycling, disco dancing, jogging, rowing, swimming and digging the garden. (Knew there'd be a catch in it somewhere.)

Walking is the simplest. And the most important thing is to start. (How *does* he do it?)

It can be difficult after years of sitting around in chairs, cars, buses and trains; being carried upwards and downwards by elevators and escalators and literally not walking more than a hundred yards in any given day.

But, as the old Chinese proverb has it: 'A journey of a thousand miles starts with the first step.' (Just mind you don't fall down it, that's all.)

Start by giving up artificial aids. Leave the car at home for short trips. Walk to the shops, walk to the station, walk to the pub.

OK, you might not like leaving the car at home. You paid a lot for that car. You spend a lot of money and time keeping it in good repair and gleaming. You want people to know you've got it.

So stick a label on your back, or get a T-shirt printed:

I'VE LEFT
THE PORSCHE
AT HOME

If you're big enough — and if you are, you certainly *should* be walking — you can add:

— AND THE
FERRARI'S IN
FOR SERVICE

Once you've done that, who needs a car anyway?

If you live close enough, walk to work. In the rush hour, you'll probably make it not much later than you would on a crowded bus. And you'll arrive, instead of with a stoop and a coughing fit, with a healthy glow. And a coughing fit.

Walk upstairs to the office instead of taking the lift. Take it in easy stages if you like: walk up to the first floor and catch the lift there. After a few days of that, walk up to the second floor and catch the lift. (If your office is on the 47th floor, you may have to call a halt somewhere. See how you feel.)

Walk *down* the stairs whenever you can: you're still stretching yourself, even though you do have gravity on your side. (Denizens of the 47th floor are again excused: you may pick up so much speed whizzing round and round the stairwell that at the bottom you screw yourself into the ground.)

Try to get in a few minutes' walking every lunchtime, if it's only going round the block twice before you turn into the pub or snack bar.

Try to make the walks interesting: a brisk stroll through the park is enough to show what you've been missing all these years.

No park? The dullest or dirtiest area can be interesting if you lift your eyes. All those bits of architecture you've never noticed before: cornices, mouldings, weathercocks, balconies, interesting bits of ironwork.

Don't keep your eyes lifted for too long at a stretch or you might discover other interesting bits of ironwork (i.e. lamp posts) by walking into them. Bad for the figure. Especially around the nose.

Anyway, get the idea? Especially if you're shy, walking is ideal. You don't have to dress up just to walk about. You don't have to stay any kind of course if you've had enough. Nobody knows what you're up to. Secret Slimmer, that's you.

Even if you don't start out too briskly, you'll soon speed up. You'll be striding out at weekends, too, exploring your own neighbourhood. Surprising how little you knew about the place. (So *that's* where they built the ballistic missile site. Only half a mile from your front door. My, my . . .)

* * *

That's got you started, anyway. You'll be surprised how soon the feeling of well-being creeps over you, and how you actually look forward to walking farther and more often. Soon you'll be feeling fit enough to try the more strenuous forms of exercise such as hill walking, jogging or swimming.

The great thing is to ease into it. Any doubts at all, see the doc. More than likely he'll pronounce you fit to start — and, what's more, be immensely relieved that at last you're on your feet.

There's an indelicate Yorkshire pub expression: 'It's bums that keep seats' — meaning that the only way to reserve a bar stool or chair is to sit on it.

Looking at it another way — and it's often not a pretty sight — it's seats that keep bums. There's only one infallible first step towards getting rid of a big end — get off it.

CHAPTER ELEVEN

Anyone for Exercise?
2: Getting in First

And now . . . What you've all been waiting for, did you but know it. Some exercises which cost you little or no physical effort, but which will help you drop the pounds painlessly. Well, almost.

Fattisthenics, they're called. For want of a better word. And they're preventive exercises: simple movements which can be developed into reflex actions to stop you taking on excess calories in the first place. They're designed to be used at four big points of contact with temptation:

The table
The food adverts
The shop and supermarket
The pub

The pub? Of course, the pub. There are more calories swilling around on a bar top than on the average dining table.

It's not uncommon for men to knock back five or six pints of beer in a session and walk out — OK, lurch out — with a thousand or more calories than they came in with.

Naturally, this doesn't happen to women. They're more refined in their habits. Perhaps demurely sipping just five teensy-weensy cocktails the whole evening. Which could leave them stacked up with 1,500 — repeat, 1,500 — surplus calories.

Of course, the pub.

Anyway, let's get on with it.

* * *

A Thousand Times No

When you're offered another helping of grub, shake your head firmly from side to side.

Eyes Front

Keep your eyes on your own plate at the table: never mind what's on anybody else's. Don't let them roam over what's left in the tureens. Don't let them run down a restaurant menu as far as the fattening desserts. And never let them swivel sideways to the gateaux trolley.

Eyes Closed
There's more about this in Chapter Four (All in the Mind), but start practising now.

Whenever you see a tempting picture of food in a magazine, close your eyes firmly. Do the same with television commercials, but this time stick a finger firmly in both ears. Advanced students can attempt to change channels with their toes.

Push Away
While you've still got room for more, push your chair away from the table. It's not a new idea — it goes back at least as far as the 12th-century philosopher Moses Maimonides, and he was as thin as a rail.* It's not easy. But it's the best exercise anybody's come up with yet.

The Window Shopping Shuffle
Unless you *have* to go in, keep on walking straight past confectioners' or sweet shops. Better still, cross the road before you get to them. Take your mind off food, or at least put yourself off your grub, by window shopping at a surgical appliance maker's or funeral parlour. (Just think: the funeral parlour depends heavily for custom on people who *don't* walk past cake shops or sweet shops.)

Should you find yourself looking into a store window containing mixed displays, close your eyes firmly at the first sight of an eclair or chocolate box and take three or four paces to the side until you can open them on to something either healthy or unappealing. (Try the do-it-yourself or hardware display. Nobody so far has been turned on by bags of cement or rolls of roofing felt. At least, nobody who was allowed to go home afterwards.)

The Supermarket Sidestep
Keep a mental plan of the supermarket layout in your head so that you can turn the trolley aside before you get to the shelves holding the gooey stuff. The detours you make could easily double the walking you do.

It's not always possible to avoid temptation, so when your trolley's full, check it over. Sort out all the fattening foods and put them back. (That's an undemanding walking, bending and stretching routine, but its real value lies in the fact that you're leaving potential fat behind you.)

You won't like parting with the food, but just add up the money you've saved. And the amount of blubber you won't be putting on. *Now* say it wasn't worth the effort.

* No? OK then, prove it.

The Demon Drink

Alcohol is packed with calories. One pint of draught bitter or pale ale holds 180 of the things; a bottle of stout, 200. Dry cider, often mistakenly thought of as 'slimming' is just as bad: 200 calories in a pint. And sweet cider — wait for it — 240.

Switching to wine and spirits does cut down the liquid intake, but you don't get away with the calories. A glass of dry wine holds 90; a glass of sweet, 115. A single measure of whisky holds 60; brandy, 75. Tiny liqueurs can notch up 90. And cocktails pack in between 115 and a horrifying 300.

Cocktails would lose a lot of their appeal if, instead of names like *Manhattan Magic, Lively Lady* or *Raving Romeo,* they were called *Zeno's Zip Zapper, Geronimo's Girdle Grinder* or *Broadway Bra Buster.*

('You look like a Bra Buster to me, darlin'. Ouch! What was *that* for?')

The great temptation is the neighbourhood pub or the city bar: warm, cosy, friendly: all the encouragement you need to relax and drink more than you should. So the following exercises are designed to help you drink less without missing out too much on the sociability.

Once they would have been aimed mainly at men. But pubs and bars are not the exclusive male preserve they once were, nor do many women think it unladylike to get stuck into a pint. So don't skip this bit, girls. Remember:

Lips that touch liquor
Make other bits thicker.

Keep Walking

Before you get to the pub, cross to the other side of the road. Keep your eyes straight ahead. And keep on walking.

You may succumb to temptation at a pub farther down the road, but at least you've burned up a few more calories, upped your metabolic rate a few metas, or possibly bolics, and not left time enough to make a beast of yourself.

Better by Half

Once inside the pub, drink halves instead of pints. Although you lose out on the calorie expenditure occasioned by lifting the heavier pint glass, you will have drunk less by closing time. Remember: just one pint less is 180 calories less.

With a half-pint glass you tend to sip, rather than sup, slurp or quaff. And you have to get served twice as often. With the speed of the service in the average pub, it means you spend a total of about half-an-hour waiting to catch the barmaid's eye, waiting again while she finishes her chat at the other end of the bar, repeating your order several times until she hears it above the din, and waiting again for her mental processes to get to grips with the change. ('Let's see, duckie. That's 40p and you gave me a 50p piece. Forty from 50 is . . .')

The frustrated hopping up and down while you're waiting for her to finish all this will push up your metabolic rate still farther. The hopping is also a way of easing the frustration, which otherwise would send your blood pressure through the roof. Blood pressure you wouldn't have if you weren't overweight.

If you're on spirits, make them small ones and dilute them, either with water or a slimline mixer. Insist on pouring the mixers yourself, for the exercise, and pour them slowly.

Give the drink a vigorous swizzle. A swizzle stick is best for this. (End of the day's original thought.) In the absence of a swizzle stick, use your finger. (In the pursuit of fitness there's no room for niceties. You can always give a sop to etiquette by sticking out your little finger as you drink: just as you do when swigging tea from the saucer.) Swizzling is not entirely necessary, but it burns up 0.000025 of a calorie or so, and fills in a bit more time.

Nary a Nibble

A danger in the pub almost as great as the booze is the array of free nibbles laid out on the bar: most of them jam-packed with calories and carbohydrates.

They've not been placed there out of the goodness of the

management's heart. Most of them are savoury and/or hold a fair amount of salt: they're there simply to increase the customers' thirsts, and are a triple hazard. They're fattening to eat, make you drink more than you intended, and the extra salt helps to retain surplus liquid in the body.

The first exercise is to push the nibbles out of reach. The second is to turn your back on them: it's asking a lot of anybody's willpower to sit staring at trays of goodies which are being wolfed the while by others less determined and figure conscious than yourself.

If you must eat something, try a beer mat. They're full of fibre and, with a dab of mustard, not bad at all. The plainer ones are best: too much printer's ink could bring on your thirst again.

Bore First, Bore Fast

Boredom is one of the big dangers. If you're bored, you drink faster.

So don't stand there on your own, nor allow yourself to get cornered by one of the pub bores. Take positive action: stride purposefully across the room and bore somebody else.

The up-and-down movement of the jaw as you expound your latest theories on the origins of the universe, the grip on the boree's lapel as you hold fast to prevent his escape, are using up calories all the time.

Not only that: while you're talking, you're not drinking. And while you're gripping his lapel, you can't get to the bar for another. (Neither can he, but he should be grateful for the good it's doing him.)

Made in Heaven

A married woman's greatest slimming aid in the pub is a husband. Unless they're newly-wed and still in the lovey-dovey stage, in which case nothing is too good for her.

But once a marriage has matured, which generally takes about three months, the average husband develops the 'What? Not *another*?' syndrome, which keeps her consumption well below the danger mark.

She gets plenty of exercise, too, at closing time. Picking him up, dusting him down, and helping him out of the pub.

But eligible single girls (or eligible married ones out on their own — nobody's said what they're eligible *for*) are in danger of having drinks thrust upon them by unscrupulous males with lustful intent.

The firm head shake is recommended here. Plus the firm slap to the wrist, punch to the throat, or knee to the naughty bits should the ardent swain reinforce his verbal pressure with persuasive gestures such as an imploring grope of the upper thigh.

There's no worry about insufficient exercise in these situations. The close combat in the back of the car later on is usually a strenuous enough workout for anybody.

None for the Road

It's usually men who succumb to the offer of One for the Road. Women have more willpower, not to say more to lose.

Use the firm side-to-side head shake again. Place your hand on top of your glass further to demonstrate your firmness of intent, and to prevent your would-be-benefactor slipping in a stiff double when you're not looking.

Should he persist, as people often do towards closing time, offer some serious-sounding excuse such as, 'Sorry, old son. Love to, but I'm on the tablets. Don't mix well with this stuff.'

If this fails, use the ultimate deterrent: the Insult. 'Sorry, old son, but one more and I'll develop a pot belly like yours.'

This could result in fisticuffs, but just think of the calorie expenditure involved in that. And even the odd missing tooth counts towards a weight loss.

The Case of the Purloined Knickers

The muffled tones of Big Ben, striking the hour, boomed dully through the thick night fog which swirled along Baker Street. (This was in the days before the horseless carriage, when Big Ben could be heard in Baker Street, even through the thick night fog.)

In the drawing room of 221b, Sherlock Holmes sat meditatively after his evening fix. The long, delicate fingers of his left hand wandered idly over the strings of the Stradivarius which lay on the carpet beside the chaise longue, and plucked out the plaintive strains of an ancient Tibetan yak-upping chant. Almost absently, he addressed the portly figure sitting opposite.

'I'm glad you dropped in, Watson. Just before you arrived, I had a communication on the electric telephone.' (Apparently this was not before the days of the electric telephone. You've got to draw the line somewhere.) 'It was Sir Geoffrey. He and Lady Penelope returned from the theatre tonight to discover that their town house had been burgled.'

'I say!' exclaimed the good doctor, his bulky thighs tensing in his tweeds. 'What bally awful luck!'

'Indeed. It was the servants' night off, so the identity of the criminal can be determined only through my supernormal powers of deduction. Come, my dear fellow. We shall investigate at once.'

'Shall I call a cab?' asked the doctor.

'Hardly necessary, my dear chap. As you will recall, they only live next door but one.'

Holmes strode through the fog with Watson puffing half a dozen paces behind.

'You really must do something about your physical condition, old chap,' said Holmes. 'Too much indulgence in port and cigars, I would say.'

'Please remember, Holmes, that your legs are longer than mine,' wheezed Watson.

'That fact had not escaped my notice,' said Holmes, peeved at what seemed to be a slight upon his powers of observation and memory, and pulled at the bell of 225b. (Electric bells were still a thing of the future.)

Twenty minutes later, after a tour of the house in the company of an agitated Sir Geoffrey and distraught Lady Penelope, Homes sat by the fire, filling his pipe with his special blend of latakia and ganja.

'Please Holmes,' said Sir Geoffrey. 'I can see you have the answer. Pray do not keep us in suspense any longer.'

Doctor Watson also appeared to be in a state of suspense. Beads of sweat stood out on his ruddy forehead and his open, candid face bore an expression of intense anticipation.

'All in good time, my dear sir,' said the Master. 'First, consider the facts.

'The pattern of the burglary, and the nature of the stolen articles, are, to say the least, unusual. From the laundry room were purloined some intimate effects of your lady wife's nether garments. From the bathroom, a bottle of your coconut oil hair restorer. From the pantry, a Swiss roll from the bottom shelf and a box of biscuits from the middle shelf. From the top shelf, which held a wide assortment of sweetmeats, eclairs and meringues, nothing was taken.

'The Swiss roll and the biscuits were consumed by the intruder as he sat on the chair in your study: the pile of crumbs in front of the chair indicates this most clearly. During this time he managed to break one of the chair legs and strain the joints of the back and the arms.

'Before or after disposing of the comestibles, he broke open the drawer of your desk and stole your private collection of Gallic visual erotica or, as they are vulgarly termed, filthy postcards.

'Finally, what seemed at first the most puzzling clue of all, but which really clinched the whole business: the scrawling on your study wall, at a height of up to four feet seven inches above the ground, a series of pencilled inscriptions in either a foreign language or an indecipherable script.

'We are looking, gentlemen and lady, for — '

At this point the atmosphere was electric. (Electric atmospheres had been around for a long time.) The silence as Holmes paused to re-light his pipe was broken only by the ticking of the clock and the heavy breathing of Doctor Watson.

' — a short, baldheaded, overweight sex maniac.'

'Moriarty!' exclaimed Watson.

'Hardly, my dear fellow. Moriarty is tall, long-haired and almost cadaverous as to physical proportions. What his sexual proclivities are I cannot hazard a guess.'

'But how,' interjected Sir Geoffrey, 'do you arrive at the description of the person in the first place?'

'I should have thought the conclusions to be self-evident,' said Holmes. 'However. First, his physical proportions. You will remember that the pantry was ransacked only on the bottom and middle shelves. The top shelf, which held even more tempting items of food, was untouched. The inscriptions in the study went to a height no greater than four feet seven inches. These facts indicate a person of modest stature.

'The assumption that he is overweight, a likely possibility in view of the theft and consumption of the biscuits and Swiss roll — and an indication of his day-to-day predilections in regard to food — is confirmed by the breaking of the leg and straining of the joints of the chair in which he sat for but a little while.

'The assumption that he is a sex maniac, or at least has some form of deviation, is indicated by the theft of Lady Penelope's nether garments and of your continental erotica.'

Watson's gasp was accompanied by an exclamation of 'Amazing!' from Sir Geoffrey.

'But how,' asked the good knight 'do we apprehend the fellow? How can we identify him positively from the hundreds of short, baldheaded, overweight sex maniacs in which London abounds?'

'This is where we return to our final clue,' said Holmes. 'The writing on the wall. It had me puzzled for a while because I was looking for an esoteric solution, such as a foreign language or long-forgotten script. Then I realised that I should accept instead a simpler solution — that the man had atrocious handwriting. Once I did this I could read the text with no difficulty whatsoever.

'It was the handwriting, gentlemen, of a medical man!'

'Then you mean — ?' exclaimed Sir Geoffrey.

'Yes! Watson, you will have the goodness to accompany me to West End Central Police Station. I should point out that, because of your deplorable physical condition, resistance would be useless.'

'In all the long years of our association, you have never ceased to astound me,' said Watson, as the hansom cab jolted towards West End Central. 'Now that our association is about to end, I must express my unbounded admiration for your exposure of my villainy from those few slender clues.'

'There were others,' said Holmes, modestly. 'The trail of knickers, camisoles and biscuit crumbs along the pavement of Baker Street from number 225b to 221b. The traces of Swiss roll in your moustache. And the sepiatone illustrated missives protruding from your top pocket, depicting scenes and events which appear to have little to do with the leisure activities of our own dear Queen. Only one thing still puzzles me.'

'And what is that?' asked Watson.

'The inscription on the wall,' said Holmes. 'Who *is* this fellow Kilroy?'

CHAPTER TWELVE

Drastic Diets

'Doctor, I'd like to diet.'

'Certainly, madam. What colour?'

No apologies for that feeble and ancient joke. If a diet were announced which involved drinking a can of paint every day, someone would try it. One recent diet, in fact, was based on seven different colours of food — one colour for every day of the week. Few of the dieters could have looked forward to Indigo Day.

Hundreds of diet fads appear every year. Each is taken up by thousands of hopeful fatties, and then dropped. This proliferation of diets is an attempt by interested parties to keep the operation fresh and interesting: to encourage people to have another go.

As you read this, one in six people in the West are on a diet, and the odds are that they'll fail. For those who want to lose about nine pounds, the failure rate is 75 per cent. Those wanting to lose 40 pounds have a failure rate of 95 per cent.

Sad, but if they'd just start eating properly and stretch their legs regularly, they wouldn't need to be on a diet in the first place.

Most diets have an inbuilt snag of one kind or another. They're boring, perhaps. Complicated. Socially awkward. Difficult or inconvenient to cook. Unappetising. Lacking in vitamins. But none of them so bad as to put people completely off their food.

That's what's been missing. Some Impossible Diets. Some Utterly Revolting and Useless Diets. So revolting, useless or expensive that the very thought of them will ruin your appetite. Every time you feel the craving coming on, look up one of the following.

For God's sake don't try them: just *think* about them. Sorry to be a bore, but there's always *somebody* daft enough . . .

The Astronauts' Diet

Developed by NASA to help astronauts acclimatise themselves to living on other planets, this diet is based on a mixture of minerals discovered on the Moon and canal water from Mars.

Tests at Houston on astronaut volunteers registered body weight losses of as much as 60 per cent in six weeks. Scientists are working on cures for side effects, which include a height reduction of 75 per cent, the turning of the skin pigment to a sickly green, the growth of three extra legs and a secondary head.

The physical changes, especially the height loss, have affected the astronauts' home life. Their wives keep complaining that they get under their feet.

The Banana Diet

Twenty bananas a day for a fortnight. Nothing else except water. You don't lose weight from the diet, but from the exercise you get climbing trees.

Side effects include involuntary beating of the chest, an addiction to old Fay Wray movies, and an irresistible urge to climb the Empire State Building.

(The most intensive, though involuntary, banana diet was that undertaken in 1978 by Senor Jose Ramon Del Cuet, Mayor of a Mexican town. So bad was he as Mayor, that 4,000 citizens stormed the town hall and made him resign, forcing him to eat 12lb of bananas before he did so. Unfortunately, nobody kept a check on his weight.)

The Carrot and Lettuce Diet

Nothing for a fortnight but raw carrots and lettuce. The weight disappears rapidly and your eyesight improves tremendously.

Side effects include cravings for saucers of bran and tea leaves. Wearing hats can be difficult because of your long, furry ears. There is a tendency to go hoppity-hop from place to place and to develop a twitch at the end of the nose. You may stop complete strangers in the street to ask, 'Nyarh . . . What's up, Doc?'

Oh, and your sexual appetite verges on the disgusting.

The Cheese Diet

Any kind of cheese you like — Cheddar, Cheshire, Edam, Brie, Stilton, Gorgonzola, Danish Blue — and as much as you like at any time you like.

Side effects include an irrational fear of cats and a tendency to nibble holes in the skirting board. If anybody asks, 'Are you a man or a mouse?' you are likely to reply, 'Eek, eek.'

The Coconut Diet

As many coconuts as you can eat. Providing you swallow them whole.

The Dripping Diet

An ancient Chinese weight-reducing regime, akin to the water torture. Nothing but dripping for every meal until you have lost 14lb in weight. This method was so successful of old that it gave rise to the ancient Chinese proverb: 'Constant dripping wears away a stone.'

The Fish Diet

One pound of raw fish for every meal will soon give you a glossy skin and a streamlined shape. You will then have only to resist a tendency towards balancing balls on the end of your nose, applauding yourself and shouting, 'Oink! Oink! Oink!'

The High Protein Diet

Very popular among overweight superstars, millionaires, belted earls and duffed-up dukes. Guaranteed to slim you right down in a matter of weeks.

Eat only food with a high protein value. Steak, lobster, crab, salmon, eggs, veal, prawns, chicken, venison, eel, grouse.

When the ordinary high protein foods start to pall, look around for scarcer forms to tempt the jaded palate. Do not be afraid to try such delicacies as ant sweetbreads, humming bird gizzards, snail tripe, smoked tadpole, Bombay ducks' parsons' noses, minced mo (the mo is an endangered species, which is why mohair coats are so expensive), devilled dodo's doodahs and ptarmigan's ptoes (ptinned).

Even stores such as Harrods and Fortnum & Mason do not stock such rarities as a matter of course, and you may have to resort to having them flown in daily by refrigerated jet.

The cost of all this is an important factor in the diet: by the time you have been on it a fortnight you will be flat broke and unable to afford to eat at all.

More than one slimmer on an exclusively high protein diet has been observed on the Embankment, accosting passers-by with pleas of 'Spare a tenner, Guv'nor, for a Poached Salmon Siberienne avec Caviare Noire et Escargots en Sauce de Courvoisier avec . . .'

The Water Diet

Ten pints of water every hour. The exercise you then get from running up and down stairs will shed pounds.

Have a regular medical check for floating kidneys. Don't worry about contracting water on the brain. That can be cured by a tap on the head.

The Spinach Diet

Spinach and nothing else, three times a day. Full of vitamins and iron. Very healthy and muscle building.

Side effects, apart from vitamin poisoning and chronic rusting, include a gravel voice, rolling gait, a tendency to sing sea shanties, to smoke a corncob pipe and a yearning to have anchors tattooed on your forearms and a sailing ship on your chest. Which can be embarrassing if you're a girl.

The Cascara and Senna Pods Diet
Cascara and senna pods are added to the basic Water Diet. The results are roughly the same, except that your sprinting speed improves. Whether or not you lose weight, at least you get a run for your money.

SOME ETHNIC DIETS

The Aborigine Diet
The Australian Aborigine lives in some of the most inhospitable country on earth, i.e. Australia, but survives by making full use of everything even remotely edible. He has a high protein diet which includes lizards, snakes, caterpillars, grasshoppers, witchetty grubs, maggots, spiders and the occasional wallaby, wombat dingbat or dongbat.

Some of these creatures are difficult to come by outside Australia, but those of us not privileged to live there can find perfectly acceptable substitutes in our own gardens and hedgerows.

Try a caterpillar pâté, an earwig mousse, scrambled daddy longlegs, worm waffles, spiders à la Incey Wincey, toad in the hole (imitation hole, real toad), slugs and snails and puppy dogs' tails in a tempting rat spleen sauce.

Then see what you fancy for afters.

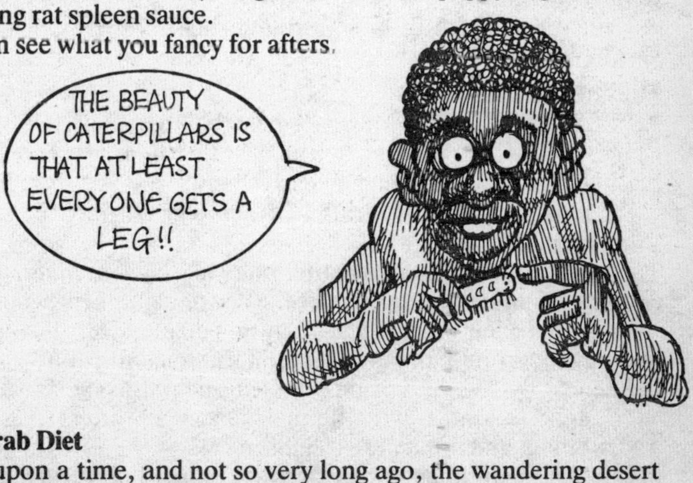

The Arab Diet
Once upon a time, and not so very long ago, the wandering desert Arabs lived a hard and spartan life. They kept fit by chasing Foreign Legionnaires and knocking hell out of each other as extras in films about Beau Geste and Lawrence of Arabia.

In spite of this, and their diet of almost nothing but mutton and goat's meat, they were very hospitable and would reserve the delicacies for their guests. The delicacies being sheep's eyeballs, staring unwinking from the communal dish.

The guests, being then almost always wandering desert anthropologists, were used to the eyeball scene. They would thank the host most profusely in his own language, make a great play of swallowing the eyeball and give the traditional belch as a mark of appreciation. The eyeball, in fact, was surreptitiously palmed, to be dropped later in the nearest oasis.

This led over the years to a lot of thin anthropologists and to the misconception that sheep's eyeballs were good for the figure. Which gets us nowhere, except to the fact that if you restrict yourself to a diet of sheep's eyeballs and hide them away until you can drop them into an oasis, you will lose weight at a hell of a lick.

Times, alas, have changed. With the sudden prosperity brought about by oil revenues, the sheikhs have gone right off eyeballs and are offering their guests more exotic delicacies.

The desert today is thronged with fat anthropologists and rolypoly Arabs, who have got that way as a result of knocking back slabs of bread pudding, spotted dick, savoury rissoles, jam sponge, treacle tart, bubble and squeak, crinkly chips and fried bread. All flown in daily by refrigerated jumbo jet to wherever the caravans are resting.

Health farms are doing a roaring trade among the dunes. Taking in rich Arabs for a fortnight at a time. And giving them nothing to eat but sheep's eyeballs.

The Eskimo Diet

As much as you can eat. Of whale meat, blubber, seal liver, bear fat, walrus giblets, sea elephant's trunk, husky chops, caribou kidney, mashed moss and shredded lichen. All raw.

As much as you can drink. Of ambergris, lamp oil, strained seaweed juice.

This diet is one of the most fattening in the world, and you are allowed to indulge at any time of the day or night. Few people do.

In an extreme emergency, such as being cut off in a blizzard without food, the Eskimo is sometimes forced to eat his canoe — the *kayak*. Because it is made from seal and walrus skins fastened to a whalebone frame with animal sinews, it offers reasonable nourishment and some fibre roughage.

The emergency has to be extremely extreme, however: without his kayak the Eskimo could come to a sticky end later on.

Hence the tragic story in Eskimo folklore of the hunter who was lost and starving on an ice floe in a blizzard. Desperate and crazed with hunger, he decided that there was nothing for it but to eat his kayak.

As he drew his hunting knife to carve out a piece of hide, a thunderous voice came from the swirling skies.

'DON'T!' it cried.

'Who are you, O Mighty One?' asked the trembling Eskimo.

'I am Big Toofypegs, the Walrus God!' thundered the voice. 'And I warn you not to touch that kayak!'

'It's all right for you,' replied the Eskimo. 'But I'm starving.'

So saying, he plunged his knife into the craft, cut off a huge chunk and gobbled it up, thankful that he still had all his teeth.

For weeks he survived on nothing but the hide of his canoe, and even got to like it.

Finally the blizzard cleared. 'At last,' thought the Eskimo. But — horror of horrors — the ice floe had shrunk to almost nothing and was drifting in rough seas far from land. The one thing that could have saved him — the kayak — was gone. Nothing but a few well-chewed spars lay on the ice.

'O Big Toofypegs! O Mighty One!' cried the Eskimo. 'Had I but listened to you! Save me!'

'Not on your life!' thundered the voice from the sky. 'And don't say I didn't warn you. Everybody knows that you can't eat your kayak and have it too . . .'

The Masai Diet

The Masai people of Kenya have long been acclaimed as among the most beautiful, courageous, lean and physically fit ethnic groups in the world. This is due to their diet of fresh blood and their hobby of chasing lions.

Cut out all solid foods and try just a cupful of blood three times a day.

Within a week or so you will have turned into a slim and superb physical specimen. All you will then have to cope with is being arrested for running around in a loincloth, making a spectacle of yourself, and spearing the local pussycats.

The Dracula Diet

Similar to the Masai diet, except that the blood is human and taken only after dark. Very popular in Transylvania and guaranteed to make you look younger and stay undead longer.

The blood mustn't be any old blood: it has to be from the jugular vein of a virgin. Things being what they are these days, most slimmers using this method tend to go down with galloping malnutrition after the first week. Perhaps they're better off for virgins in Transylvania.

CHAPTER THIRTEEN

Roughing It

The diets in the previous chapter will have filled a long felt want or two. If you have any felt wants left, save them for the Fibre Diet. Long felt wants are best, but even short ones are full of roughage.

The Fibre Diet, which is certainly not useless and not very revolting — unless you are caught unawares by a possibly explosive after-effect — is lately back in vogue, but has long been recommended by dieticians and health specialists.

Plenty of fibre in your food is the secret. Not only is it an eminently sensible diet, it allows much more variation than most of the others. It's not expensive and it never leaves you with that sinking feeling. (What it does leave you with, we'll come to later.)

Adolf Hitler was one of the early pioneers of the fibre diet, if the stories are to be believed about his habit of chewing the carpet every time he flew into a rage.

'Roughage' is what our parents called it, and it includes the stuff which food manufacturers go to enormous trouble to take out of our food. Many of them are now going to equally enormous trouble to make sure it stays in. Either that or they're packaging it separately as a slimming aid: which means you're paying good money for bran to balance the doughy white loaf you're eating — bran which was taken out of the loaf in the first place.

Fibre, then, includes the husks of cereals which are often taken out in the milling process to leave white flour and polished rice. There is also plenty in beans, peas, green leaf vegetables, fruit and nuts. It's the stuff which kept our primitive ancestors slim. Not to mention regular.

The former bogies of slimming diets — bread and potatoes — are now recommended as rich in fibre, especially if the bread is wholemeal, the potato is baked in its skin, and neither is cooked or eaten with butter or fat.

There are other sources of bulk fibre: doormats, beermats, coconut husks, cotton waste, Harris tweed jackets, shredded newspapers, cereal packets, and ready-bagged forms such as peat or bark which you can get from any garden centre. For some reason, these forms of fibre have never achieved much popularity. Something to do with the marketing, perhaps.

(This book, incidentally, is packed with fibre. If all else fails, eat it. If you enjoy it, tell your friends.)

Benefits claimed for a fibre diet are many. It prevents constipation and other connected disorders, including piles and a nasty-type bowel inflammation called diverticulitis. It is also claimed to help prevent diabetes and heart disease.

Its chief help in slimming, apart from the fact that fibre itself is not fattening, is that it goes through the digestive system at a hell of a speed. It absorbs water, swells, makes the stomach feel full, and gives the intestines something to get hold of. More than that: for some reason it takes with it a lot of potential energy from other foods which would otherwise get absorbed into the system to lay up fat.

This energy, then (and squeamish readers stop squeaming and read on) is passed from the body in what are, in effect, high-calorie stools. It seems a waste. It *is* a waste — but you can't complain if you're eating too much, which is waste anyway.

Obviously the Fibre Diet holds a couple of social drawbacks. All that bulk in your intestines makes its presence felt. When you've got to go, you've got to go. But that's much better than writhing for days in the throes of constipation.

The other main drawback is flatulence. (The *Blazing Saddles* syndrome.) Which is why the Wide Open Spaces were wide open. It's a very healthy side effect, and one which shows the diet's working, but it can be embarrassing in polite company.

'How dare you break wind in front of my wife?'

'I'm terribly sorry. I didn't know it was her turn.'

Very soon the dieter learns to control the flatulence, or to relieve it in circumstances of solitariness. (Even in a crowd it's amazing how quickly you become solitary.) But meanwhile it must lead to some changes in procedure at health and slimming club gatherings.

The toastmaster at a Fibre Club celebration dinner must have to modify his call to order: 'Pray silence — or at least stop talking . . .' He may even have to take the blame for the rumblings of the guest speaker, interjecting at embarrassing moments with: 'My lords, ladies and gentlemen. *Mea culpa.* A thousand apologies. Pray carry on, Your Royal . . .'

To save the toastmaster from accepting too much of the blame, husbands of lady members may have to take on the role of scapegoat, apologising and blushing madly at each raspberry from the next seat. Richer members, of course, will be able to hire complete strangers — resting actors, perhaps — to take the rap.

Certainly at such gatherings there will be no smoking until after the dessert — and then only after all the doors and windows have been flung open wide — if the proceedings are not to end with a bang.

Methane — the gaseous by-product of a fibre diet — is highly inflammable and, mixed with air, explosive. A British magazine Agony Aunt advised her readers that a match struck after going to the loo would clear the air to the extent that nobody would ever know you'd been.

Sound and safe enough advice. But try striking a match in a really high concentration of methane. People would know you'd been, all right. But they might never know where you'd got to.

The gas is known in nature as marsh gas, and in industry as the deadly firedamp of the coalmines. Fibre clubs could ensure the safety of their meetings by using the old miners' method of diagnosing a dangerous build-up of gas: a canary in a cage. If the canary falls off its perch, nobody strikes a match.

Methane has been put to good use, however, by pioneers of clean fuel who have used it to power trucks and cars. The cost of a fibre club outing could be cut enormously by using a methane-powered motor coach. Whatever else, the fuel would certainly be lead-free. And there'd be no worries about running out of gas. As the gauge hit the red marker, the driver would only have to turn round and shout: 'Right, folks! All together now . . .'

* * *

More long-term and serious effects of fibre could include heatwaves and flooding.

Scientists in Australia and the United States have noted that the level of methane gas in the atmosphere has increased considerably over recent years.

Methane traps heat reflected from the Earth's surface and creates a 'greenhouse' effect which could lead to an overall rise in temperatures, the eventual melting of polar ice caps and the flooding of low-lying areas.

The scientists are blaming it at the moment on the poor old cow, who admittedly does fart a lot. World cattle populations almost doubled between World War Two and 1982. This, say the scientists — plus a lesser rise in the number of sheep and goats — is the cause of the methane increase.

What they forget is that there are many more people than cows, and that the largest human population increase has been in the Third World, where a fibre diet already exists. Recently there's been an increase in fibre consumption in the West. The sudden increase in methane levels can't be just coincidence.

Not that the danger is great or immediate, but you never know. Insurance companies will certainly be inclined to load the fire and flood clauses on any cover for a fibre club, what with the danger from explosions, tropical climates and all that water from the polar ice caps. So organisers are advised to hold functions somewhere airy and beyond the reach of floodwater. (There has already been a sudden increase in popularity of the Mount Ararat Assembly Rooms.)

And just remember — No Smoking. Not even if the canary's on its feet. It might have got used to it.

* * *

We digress. The best way of easing social embarrassment at fibre club gatherings is to accept from the start that these things (i.e. strange noises and maidenly blushes) will happen. Perfectly natural and normal. Speakers should be prepared for it, and ready to introduce the occasional and appropriate limerick to break the ice. Such as:

A well-bred young lady named Pat
Took up fibre to rid her of fat.
At her 600th bean
She said, 'Gad, I feel mean.'
And politely machine-gunned the cat.

Or:

A husband and wife, name of Martin,
Were seriously considerin' partin'.
She said, 'Why the din?
'Don't you like me so thin?'
He said, 'No. I just can't stand you in the throes of flatulence.'

To get everybody really involved, there's nothing like a limerick competition. Try finishing this one, for instance:

There was a young lady from Cheltenham
Who liked eating chips with some felt in 'em.
By her 31st spud
She really felt good
And ....

You will have realised after half-an-hour's brain-wracking that no author offers an incomplete limerick that he'd any hope of finishing himself. Sorry about that.

(Oops! Pardon. Or was that you?)

CAUTIONARY TALES FOR FAT PEOPLE: 4

The Longest Knight

Once upon a time, in a country far away, lived a king and his slim and beautiful daughter, the Princess Peroxilocks.

It was a happy land, with lots of hard work in the fields, but lots of laughter and song at the end of the day.

'Our land is so happy,' said the king to his slim and beautiful daughter, 'it is almost too good to be true. It worries me. I'm so afraid that one day something will come along and spoil it.'

One day, something did. The fearsome Dragon Thunderbore came down from his lair in the Mountains of Doom, laying waste the farms of the happy land and burning whole fields of corn with one blast of his fiery breath.

The knights of the land rode out, one after the other, to do battle with the dragon. One after the other, the brave and noble men were slain.

'Dragon! Dragon!' cried the people. 'What can we offer to make you stop all this destruction? Our fields and our homes are being devastated every day. Soon there will be nothing left. Just tell us what you want. Whatever it is, you shall have it!'

'I will stop only if I am given enough food every day to fill seven times seven oxcarts to the brim: some with meat, some with vegetables, some with bread, some with pastries, some with the fishes of the rivers and the seas!' roared the fearsome Dragon Thunderbore.

'These must be brought to me every day at my lair in the Mountains of Doom. And to make sure there is no trickery or delay, I will take back with me your slim and beautiful Princess Peroxilocks. No harm will come to her so long as the food is brought every day. But let it once fail to arrive — !'

Thunderbore had no need to go further. The people were shocked by the demands of food and completely horrified by the thought of their beloved Princess Peroxilocks living with the dragon in his foul lair. But there was no other way. To save the lands of his people, the heartbroken king bade a tearful farewell to his only child, the slim and beautiful Princess Peroxilocks.

For a year and a day, seven times seven oxcarts of food made the long journey, seven times a week, to Thunderbore's lair in the

Mountains of Doom. There was never any sign of the Princess, but the oxcart drivers could hear her singing in the depths of the cave. They realised that the dragon, for all his ferocity, must be treating her well.

However, seven times seven oxcarts, every day for a year and a day, added up to a great deal of food. By the end of the time, the coffers of the Royal Treasury were empty. The king tried to tax the people more to pay for the food, but they cried: 'How can you tax us any more, when we are taxed so heavily already that we are nearly starving? There is only one answer — the dragon must die!'

The king brooded in his chamber. To kill the dragon, he would need a knight. But all his own knights had been slain. He dared not send out heralds to proclaim his plight in the countries beyond the happy land, offering his daughter's hand in marriage as people in his position usually did. If the dragon were to hear that he was looking for a knight, he would gobble up the slim and beautiful princess straightaway. What was a king to do?

There was a tap on the door and a servant entered. 'Sire, there is a person without who says he is a knight, and craves audience with you. Though such a knight, Sire, I never did see.'

'Never mind,' said the king. 'Send him in.'

In walked the strangest spectacle. Very tall, pale and painfully thin. The tallest and thinnest man the king had ever seen.

'Greetings, Sire,' said the apparition in a reedy, piping voice. 'Permit me to introduce myself. Sir Timothy Tinribs, Knight of the Long Shanks, Champion Dragon Killer of the Whole Wide World, at your service. I hear you have a small problem which I shall be more than happy to solve — providing I may have your slim and beautiful daughter's hand in marriage.'

'Done! Done!' cried the king, delightedly. 'By all means marry my daughter. But —' and here he paused as if in doubt — 'don't think me rude or anything, but you don't look much like a dragon killer to me.'

'Exactly,' replied the tall, thin knight. 'Nor do I look it to the dragons. I wander about in front of their lairs, wearing peasant's clothes over my armour, and pick daisies while singing simple rustic songs. The dragons think I am some half-witted peasant disturbing their nap, come out to eat me up and presto! — with a leap to the side and one stab of my trusty sword, it's all over.'

'Splendid!' exclaimed the king. 'When can you start?'

'I'm on my way, Sire,' said the knight. And off he rode.

It was easy enough to lure Thunderbore from his lair. He had just finished eating a couple of oxcarts of strawberry flans and cheesecakes and was trying to settle down for a quiet snooze. The tuneless singing from outside annoyed him, and he lumbered out to settle the hash of the tall, thin peasant he found picking daisies. So full was Thunderbore of strawberry flan and cheesecake that he could not swerve in pursuit when the peasant jumped to one side. Suddenly, with a quick stinging sensation under his left wingpit, Thunderbore was no more.

Sir Timothy wiped his sword, stripped the peasant's rags from his shining armour, and called to the cave: 'Most slim and beautiful Princess Peroxilocks! You can come out now! I have slain the dragon and you are free! I claim your slim and lilywhite hand in marriage!'

'You've done *what*? And you claim *what*?' replied an angry voice from the cave — and out stormed the fattest woman that Sir Timothy had ever seen.

It was undoubtedly Princess Peroxilocks, for no other woman in the land had hair so silky and shining as she, but she was *enormous*! She waddled over to Dragon Thunderbore, lifted his lifeless head, and laid it tenderly on her massive lap. Then she looked up at the tall, thin knight, her eyes brimming with tears.

'Do you know what you've done?' she cried. 'You've killed the kindest hearted dragon in the whole wide world. He really knew how to treat a girl. Every day there were lashings of strawberry flans, cheesecakes, roast meats, baked fish, fresh bread, huge pastries, cakes, mountains of dumplings and rivers of soup.

'Now it's all gone — thanks to you! You long streak of wind and celery water! I wouldn't marry you if you were made out of marzipan! If you were smothered in chocolate sauce! If you were stuffed with sage and onion, parsley and thyme, had an apple in your mouth and a walnut in each ear!'

She looked brokenheartedly down into her lap.

'Thunderbore,' she breathed, tenderly. 'Speak to me . . .'

There was no reply. The dragon was very, very dead.

Peroxilocks laid the huge head gently on the greensward, strode purposefully into the cave, and strode purposefully out again bearing an enormous frying pan. With a *boi-oi-oinggg*! which could be heard for miles, she bent the pan over the Long Knight's head.

The resulting fracture and dislocation of two of his thoracic vertebrae, followed swiftly by death, made it impossible for them to live happily ever after.

Which is sad, because every fairy tale should have a happy ending.

CHAPTER FOURTEEN

On the Job

Size definitely restricts choice of jobs, especially in areas where image is important. Whoever heard of a 16-stone Human Hairpin, for a start? Or a 20-stone receptionist at a health and beauty club?

To be fair, there are jobs open to people simply because they *are* fat. Jobs like sitting in a restaurant by the window, stuffing your face for free to attract the customers, would never be given to a skinny person. Nobody would pay to see an anorexic tattooed lady with room for only the bowsprit of HMS *Victory* on her chest. Nor would a five-stone belly dancer have any attractions apart from morbid curiosity about whether she'd have the strength to finish.

But there are many jobs which the overweight are physically unable to do. At 18 stone, for instance, you could never be a ballet dancer without ruining your partner's *entrechat*. No use, either, auditioning for *Peter Pan*. Even if you got the job, the lads working the flying ballet tackle would walk out in protest or demand truss money.

Not that show business doesn't offer the occasional opening for the well developed. Who could forget, for instance, the world-renowned Irish exotic dancer, Titania O'Knockers, whose measurements were 74-24-36? She never even had to dance, let alone strip. All she did was to lie down on the stage and try to get up. Or Tessie Tubfull, the 22-stone stripper? Every night she finished her act to deafening cries of 'On! On! On!'

For every success story such as Titania's and Tessie's, however, there have been dozens in which excess weight meant failure, not to mention serious injury.

Take the sad case of Salome Tremble, one of the most accomplished tassel dancers in the western hemisphere. She was glad when her bust started to increase in size: it gave extra bravura to the part of the routine where the tassels swung first one way, then the other, and finshed up rotating in opposite directions.

There came a time, however, when the ratio of size-of-boob to arc-of-swing became critical. Salome suffered increasingly from ear damage, caused by being struck from either side at the climax of the contra-rotating routine. After six months she developed cauliflower ears. After 12 months she had to retire altogether — punch drunk and totally deaf.

Almost all the more athletic jobs in show business, in fact, are out from the start. The only fat high-wire performer the circus ever knew was 16-stone Hermione Twang, billed as *The Biggest Star Out Tonight.*

Hermione's speciality was somersaults on the high wire, and for several years she executed them without incident. But she made the mistake of not keeping a daily check on her weight. One night she appeared without realising that she was carrying another half stone.

That extra seven pounds was enough. For the climax of her act, Hermione executed her famous quadruple aeroplane spin with a jack knife and double reverse pike, ending in the splits. She landed on the wire from a great height, with a force that stretched it almost to the sawdust. With an almighty *boi-oi-oinnnnnnnng*! the wire twanged taut again, propelling Hermione like a star-spangled cannonball through the top of the tent.

She landed on the spire of St Botolph's-on-the-Water, severely damaging the weathercock and rupturing the four firemen who brought her to safety. Her career was at an end. Not only was the experience so traumatic that the very thought of a high wire brought her out in spots, but landing on the weathercock meant that she could never do the splits again.

* * *

Seriously, many employers are prejudiced against fat people. An official of a big employment agency in California claimed that the prejudice could be justified.

Fatties, she said, are often unreliable and lacking in imagination at work. 'The fat *female* employee,' she went on, adding injury to insult, 'is generally a few minutes late — always with elaborate excuses — but coffee breaks are meticulously observed.'

A Danish reform group proposed that fat people be taxed an hour's pay every month for every kilo they were overweight. And a management agency in New York estimated that every pound of overweight means a drop in income of around £500 a year.

In Britain, where employers are less likely to use the weight-for-height-scales quite so strictly, there is still some prejudice against an applicant's shape, especially at management level.

The manager of an agency for sales and marketing executives was quoted as saying: 'I would certainly look twice at a distinctly overweight person because our job area is closely tied up with image and smart appearance. A fat person hits the fatigue level quicker. But it would be silly to make rejection automatic, because recruitment is often so personal.'

'If you are fat,' said a British dietician, 'your job value in the market place goes down. Nobody wants a fat receptionist or a fat, lethargic salesman.'

And the medical officer of a top management health centre, responsible for checking applicants for boardroom positions, said: 'Obesity by itself is not the handicap: it may indicate unsuitability on other grounds. If a person is more than 10 per cent over the appropriate weight-for-height, it does raise questions of self-management and balanced outlook, as well as the familiar problems associated with excess weight.'

The assumptions are all a bit sweeping: that fat people are necessarily dozy, lacking in drive and prone to self-indulgence. Imagine some of the job interviews that could have gone on in the past:

'So you want the job as King, eh? And how do you think you're going to look at the coronation? You're absolutely bloated, man. It's not just your appetite for food — *all* your appetites are over the top. Six wives, for God's sake . . . !'

'You wish to be considered for the post of lexicographer? I hope you realise that compiling a dictionary involves method, neatness, diligence and application. Just look at yourself: grossly overweight, snuff and egg yolk all down your coat, and dandruff on your collar. Sorry, you're just not what we're looking for, Dr.—er—Johnson?'

'You're quite heavy for your height, I'm afraid, and the job does involve a lot of physical effort. You'd have to walk from Paris to Moscow, for a start. And back. I think you'd meet your Waterloo if you attempted that, especially with that stomach trouble of yours—I assume it's stomach trouble from the way you keep your hand inside your waistcoat? I hear, too, that your low fatigue threshold is giving you some personal problems. "Not tonight, Josephine," was the phrase used, I believe. Well, I *mean* . . .'

'So you intend to fight them on the beaches, do you? On the landing grounds, eh? On the sea and in the air? Taking a lot upon yourself, aren't you, at your age and your weight? I hear through the grapevine that you're rather fond of the old grog, too. A bit much at a time like this. Don't you know there's a war on . . . ?'

Not that the fatties are taking things lying down, at least not in the States, where there have been several lawsuits against employers for alleged discrimination. A 25-stone woman in Philadelphia complained that a local company had turned down her job application on the grounds of 'morbid obesity'. The court not only awarded her the job: it threw in 20,000 dollars back pay.

In Connecticut, a 24-stone policeman sued the police authority for wages lost when he failed to meet an official slimming schedule. In Pittsburg, a 17-stone woman who was sacked for failing to slim to her employers' specifications, won a court order for re-instatement in her post at the city jail. She and others have been helped by the National Association to Aid Fat Americans, which certainly gives a new meaning to heavyweight litigation.

It is a fact, though, that people in jobs can eat themselves out of them. Weight Watchers, for instance, has had members who included firemen who became too heavy to climb a ladder, machine minders too fat to get into their work spaces, professional drivers who couldn't get behind the wheel—even shipyard workers whose mates did the welding for them, because they themselves couldn't get through the hatches.

Fatties in distress can cause problems with other people's jobs, especially for emergency services, and especially now that women are claiming the right to join.

New York Fire Department signed on its first female members after a legal battle in which the women claimed that the physical tests discriminated against them. A court ordered the department to revise its tests and reserve 45 jobs for women. Among the revisions was the dragging of a 145lb dummy up and downstairs, rather than carrying a 120lb one.

But they were told by Mayor Ed Koch, as he swore them in, that the important thing was being 'able to carry a 206lb mayor out of a window'.

* * *

Not only in jobs is there discrimination against fatties. The overweight were certainly among those whom the authorities of the town of Tropes, Italy, had in mind when they banned nude sunbathers from the beaches.

Not all nude sunbathers, mind you. The municipal ordnance made an exception in the case of 'beautifully naked young women — possibly young women in a position to exalt the attractiveness and femininity of their bodies'. The ordnance was enforced by the local police, who presumably still went around insisting that their lot was not a happy one.

* * *

The cause of excess weight might be the job itself. Not only might it be completely sedentary, in which case you would need some regular exercise to counteract it, it might not be the right kind of job. Any job which gives undue pressures or worries, which bores you, or which is wrong for your temperament or personality, could start you off on compensatory eating.

If you were a kleptomaniac, for instance, you would find working in a bullion warehouse frustrating. If you could not swim, you would not be happy training dolphins. If you could not stand crowds, you might not enjoy selling programmes at football matches. If you were a compulsive nibbler, what chance would you stand in a chocolate factory? And a potential sex maniac would find temptation a little strong with a job at the YWCA. (Nymphomaniacs would be OK at the Y*M*CA. I'm sure the lads wouldn't mind.)

What kind of a job, then, would prevent your putting on weight? Leaving aside those jobs which involve contact with food, the choice is still wide. There are only two essential conditions:

(a) That the job presents a real challenge, so that plenty of time and effort have to be put in to make a success of it.

(b) That the financial rewards are not great enough to encourage spending of surplus cash on food.

These two criteria were fed into the *How To Avoid Slimming* cut-price computer, which produced the following list of the Top Twenty Suitable Occupations:

Submarine builder to the Swiss Navy
Bacon slicer salesman in Tel Aviv
Deep sea diver in the Gobi Desert
Sex shop proprietor in the Vatican
Cat doctor to the Kennel Club
Yiddisher comedian in Saudi Arabia
Shrimp boat salesman in the Himalayas
Proprietor of a philosophical bookshop in Queensland
Hod carrier on Pyramid restoration projects
Blacksmith to the Camel Corps
Trawler skipper on the Dead Sea
Flat Earth Consultant to the International Space Programme
Long distance lorry driver on Tristan da Cunha
Speech therapist at a Trappist monastery
Flag day collector in Aberdeen
Pall bearer at an elephants' graveyard
Sun lamp salesman in Sidi bel Abbes
Bra concessionaire to Women's Lib
Dry cleaner at a nudist camp
Head barman for Alcoholics Anonymous

CHAPTER FIFTEEN

Sorry About That . . .

Statistics on the incidence of accidents caused by excess weight seem not to exist. Insurance companies load their life policies because of the decreased life expectancy of the obese, and load their accident policies because 'the rate of recovery of such persons from accidental injury is impaired'.* But, they say, there is no evidence that obese people are more accident-prone than slimmer ones.

Perhaps it's one of Nature's compensatory factors. Fatties are less active, get about less, move more slowly and perhaps with more care, tend not to climb trees or mountains, and are not inclined towards such potentially dangerous pursuits as sky-diving, hang-gliding or alligator-wrestling.

But when a fatty *is* on the move, accidents *do* happen simply because of excess weight. Slim people seldom get stuck in turnstiles, automatic ticket barriers, revolving doors, baths or telephone booths. Nor do they smash their way through chairs, beds, ladders and lavatory seats.

The author knew a 19-stone captain of industry who spent the night in a tiny service lift after working late one evening. He was on his way to the ground floor when his bay-window belly pressed the emergency stop. The lift jammed between floors and stayed jammed. Because of the lateness of the hour, the building was empty and his screams for help went unheard. He wasn't found until the cleaners arrived for work next morning.

He was lucky, though. It was the night before the firm closed down for a fortnight's holiday. Had he become stuck the following night he would have emerged 14 days later — if he emerged at all — as the Institute of Directors' Slimmer of the Year.

While I'm boring you with personal reminiscences, you may as well have another. I went for a job interview when my weight had reached 13½ stone. Not massive, but nobody had told my overcoat. I strode confidently into the managing director's office, stuck out my chest and stretched out my hand for the statutory firm, executive-material handclasp.

* That's a frightener, for a start. Imagine the talk over the operating table: 'Dig a bit deeper, Carruthers. It's the spleen we're after — dammit, man, you've only just reached his navel . . .'

A button pinged off my overcoat and hit the M.D. smack on the nose.

'Thank you, Mr — er . . . er . . .' he said, blinking through watering eyes. 'And what do you do for an encore?'

('Funny,' said the wife, a fortnight later. 'You've still not heard about that job . . .')

* * *

One of the fatty's big problems is gauging the outer limits of his person, especially if the outer limits are still expanding. Here today, over there tomorrow.

The rear accounts for a lot of these problems. It will swing round in restaurants, bars, at parties and in china shops, to sweep all behind it. A fatty risks coming out of an antique shop with a bill for two dozen Meissen originals and nothing to show for it but a bagful of bits and a tube of instant glue.

Women have the extra problem of the bust. It is not unknown for matrons of statuesque proportions to swing round suddenly and lay some inoffensive passer-by unconscious on the floor.

They can attempt some sort of control with foundation garments. But the garments themselves may find the task stretching their resources too far.

There was the lady dog breeder who had put on a lot of weight and who got herself a new bra for Cruft's. But the first time she bent over at the show, the bra proved unequal to the challenge.

A shortsighted, middle-aged little man peered at the burgeoning bosoms and said, 'Excuse me. If those pups are for sale, could I have the one with the pink nose?'

It's often the bizarre quality of the accident that leaves the fatty covered in shame and blushes. And leaves everybody else falling about.

Like getting stuck in a loo seat. If the firemen can't free you on the spot, and you have to be unscrewed and carted *in situ* to the ambulance, you are bound to get waggish neighbours and bystanders doing the cross-talk bit:

'Phwarh! Ever seen one of them before?'

'Often — but never framed.'

If you get stuck in the bath, you face the prospect of several hours in water which is getting colder and colder. By the time the alarm is raised and the firemen arrive, you will have taken on an unbecoming pimply texture and turned a deep shade of blue. And if the firemen can't shift you with a soaking of soft soap or liquid paraffin, they'll have to cut the bath loose and call in the heavy squad to carry you out.

'Look at that, Jim. Cleopatra in her barge!'

'Yer. I can see what made Julius seize 'er. Har har.'

Digressing for a moment, Cleopatra could have started bathing in asses' milk in an attempt to get her weight down. She really was dumpy: there are bas-reliefs to prove it. Her bas in relief was beyond belief.

Anyway, the Asses' Milk Marketing Board had been putting it about that the stuff was a reducing agent. And she fell for it.

The head bath attendant, Mustafa Shufti, said in his high-pitched voice (he was really cut out for the job): 'How would you like the milk, ma'am — pasteurised?'

'No,' said Cleo. 'Just up to my chest.'

Mark Antony had been complaining about Cleo's weight for some time (not that he could talk: he was only 5ft 3in tall and looked like a barrel of lard) and he'd started to knock her about. That was what finally decided her to clutch an asp to her bosom. As the ancient Egyptian lament has it:

Cleo, to her friends known as Pat,
Was in trouble for running to fat.
Ere Tony could swipe 'er
She grabbed a small viper
And said, 'There you are — tit for tat.'

. . . Since we're into low comedy (not that we seem to get very far out of it) you may as well stick around for a couple or more jokes in equally doubtful taste:

A story about a jumbo-sized sporting peer of Edwardian times relates how he was run into by an early motor car.

The car got the worse of the encounter, but the peer was still very annoyed.

'What the deuce is the matter with you, man?' he raved at the driver. 'There's plenty of room. And you can't have been in that much of a hurry. Couldn't you have gone round me?'

'I had the room, my lord,' answered the motorist. 'And the time. But I didn't have the petrol.'

* * *

A winter sports enthusiast, who was far too fat for safety, came a cropper on the ski run and was visited by his friend in hospital.

'I don't quite know what happened,' he croaked. 'I was doing perfectly well, then all of a sudden I turned a somersault on the er . . . on the er . . .'

'Piste?' asked his friend.

'No,' said the shattered skier. 'I'd only had a couple of gins.'

* * *

A very fat old Yorkshireman was dying in his tiny attic bedroom, and a friend called to cheer him up.

'Don't fret, lad,' said the friend. 'We'll soon have you up and about. Just get some of that weight off and you'll be fit enough to get back in the bowls team in no time.'

'Nay, lad. I'm going,' said the old man.

'Never,' said his pal. 'Stick to that diet the wife's put you on and you'll be skipping down the road to the *Strangled Ferret* like a two-year-old. The lads are looking forward to getting you back in the darts team as well. They really miss your treble twenties.'

'No chance,' said the old boy. 'I've resigned meself to it.'

His friend talked non-stop for the next 20 minutes, all about the mates who were looking forward to seeing him back playing bowls and darts, and finally the old man cheered up.

'Ay, you're right,' he said. 'Once I've got a bit of this weight off I'll be as good as new. I'll show 'em a thing or two.'

'That's the way,' said his mate. 'Well, I've got to be going. But just think on: stay off the grub.'

He turned to go and banged his head on the lintel of the low attic doorway.

'Bloody 'ell,' he said. 'We'll never get your coffin down them stairs . . .'

* * *

One of the problems with being overweight is that you can cause accidents even after you've gone to the Great Nosh Bar in the Sky. The next two stories might sound funny, but they're absolutely true and weren't funny at the time. At least, not to anybody without a warped sense of humour.

(Tee-hee. Shurrup.)

In 1982 a Liverpool pallbearer was sacked from his job at the undertakers. His employers listed transgressions such as turning up late for services, forgetting to deliver flowers and failing to show respect in church. But what finally did it was his dropping the coffin of a 23-stone docker.

An industrial tribunal decided he had been unfairly dismissed on technical grounds (Whoops!) but that he had contributed 75 per cent to his sacking. He was awarded £1,182 compensation.

A 5ft 3in pallbearer in Leeds offered his resignation because his lack of height meant that he had to push up really hard to keep his end of the coffin at the height of the other pallbearers' shoulders and it was causing him severe muscle strain. The funeral of a local fatty, which almost dislocated his shoulder, was the last straw.

'We don't want to lose you,' said his kindly boss, asking him to reconsider his decision. 'Tell you what — in future, take the leg end of the coffin. That's always lighter.'

This he did. The leg ends were no problem. And all went well until the funeral of a man who was not only fat, but legless. On the way into the church the corpse slid down in the coffin and the pallbearer slipped a disc.

So think on . . .

CHAPTER SIXTEEN

Bigger than Both of Us

Too much weight can cause problems with your sex life. Problems with your sex life can cause you to put on too much weight. Too much weight can cause problems with your sex life. Problems with your sex life can cause you to put on too much weight. Too much weight . . .

By now you've probably got the drift. There are few circles more vicious than that of sex problems and compensatory eating.*

A lot of people with worries about sex grow fat. There is a close relationship between the hunger for sex and the hunger for food. Compensatory eating figures high among the symptoms of those who are:

(a) Not getting their share.
(b) Getting their share but not really enjoying it.
(c) Trying to avoid getting their share.

The first two categories are self-explanatory. The third is more common than you'd think. People with a conscious or unconscious fear of sex will eat to make themselves undesirable. It's better for their ego to think, 'Nobody fancies me because I'm overweight,' than 'Nobody fancies me because I'm no good in bed.' Or, worse, 'Nobody fancies me, full stop.'

If sex is the problem, it's important to admit it from the start, embarrassing or not. Of course it's upsetting to have the dietician or psychotherapist asking highly personal questions. What the hell's it got to do with them how many times a month you indulge, or attempt to? And most people tend to lie at the start, anyway: 'Oh . . . About average, I suppose . . .'

But once it's been established that the guzzling is connected with sex, or with the lack of it, the problem is a lot easier to tackle. Get the sex right, and it's easier to cut down on the food. Cut down on the food, and it's easier to get the sex right. Take the viciousness out of the circle.

* * *

* See also *How to Avoid Sex* (New English Library, £1.50). Guaranteed to put you off your grub.

There are five obstacles to the full enjoyment of sex for the overweight:

The *Yuk*! Factor
The *What*? Factor
The *Where*? Factor
The *Whoops*! Factor
and
The *Aaargh*! Factor

The *Yuk!* Factor

So called because of the exclamation given by obese lovers as they turn to view each other in their pristine glory, i.e. starkers. 'Yuk!' they cry. Perhaps, 'Groo!' Or even, 'Bleargh!'

Which does not get the Close Encounter off to the best of starts.

This factor applies to the really tubby, of course: there's nothing wrong with a *bit* of extra weight. In spite of current vogues for the unisex look, men are still turned on by the sight of a well-upholstered woman. (See *The Dolly Parton Story, or Me and My Buckled Guitar.*)

Some extra covering on the buttocks and the breasts (The Wobbly Bits, as they are known in medical circles), helps to emphasise the femininity of the figure, and certainly helps a partner to find his way in the dark.

But once the weight spreads to the waist, thighs, arms and neck, it's in competition with the genuine Wobbly Bits and makes them look less pronounced. Shame, after all the time and effort which went into growing them.

Rolls of extra fat may even be grabbed by a swain in mistake for something more interesting. It's always a disappointment for a man to find he's been going bananas over something which is not only intrinsically boring, but shouldn't even be there in the first place.

Too much fat on a man detracts even more drastically from the masculine image. It makes him look shorter, as well as rounder. Once he's lost his lean waist, sculptured shoulders and long legs, the general effect is that of an overweight baby.

This is fine for a woman who only wants to mother her loved one, but it's embarrassing for the bloke if he's got to sit there waving a rattle, sucking a dummy and doing nothing else but wait for nappy rash to set in.

Is there any way of overcoming the *Yuk*! Factor before the weight comes off? Breathing in and not breathing out can help, but you can't keep that up for long (not without turning purple and keeling over, which can take some of the romance out of the occasion). Years of research by the world's leading sexologists have produced only one short-term answer: turn out the light.

The *What!* Factor

The skinny person and the fat person both have the same number of nerve endings. The thinner you are, the closer these areas of nerve are together and the more sensitive you are to stimulation and touch. Sounds logical enough, but nobody thought of it until a British biochemist did some research into the relationship between size and sex. He discovered also that thin people are more sexually aggressive and active than fatties.

So not only do you get more of it if you're skinny, you enjoy it more while you're getting it.

It is possible for fatties to ensure that they cover all the sensitive areas by the old piece-of-chalk method. You hug your loved one and make a chalk mark at the extremity of the hug. You hug the next bit, make another chalk mark, and so on. The essence of simplicity, it makes sure that nothing's missed out. But the process is often spoiled, as is related in song and story, by meeting somebody else who's hugging and chalking the other way.

The *Where!* Factor

A British fertility specialist warned fatties that surplus weight could make them unable to stay the course in their love lives. The cause, he said, was 'the surplus fat that oozes between all the tissues'. (*Oozes* . . . Nothing like a well-chosen word to put you off.)

But read on. 'Every internal organ is embedded in adipose tissue, upsetting its activity,' he continued. 'The genital organs and the muscles that control them are no exception and are unable to perform normally. This is quite apart from the problem of locating them beneath the rolls of fat.'

So not only isn't the thing working properly, but you couldn't even find it if it were. It gives a new meaning to the seaside postcard caption, 'Have you seen my little Willy?'

And certainly it's true that a fat man's pride and joy looks smaller than a thin man's, simply because part of it is buried in a roll of fat. Little things may mean a lot, and all that, but there are limits.

The *Whoops!* Factor

Fatties are accident prone in most strenuous activities. Sex has a higher risk factor than most — even if you discount collapsing beds and simple suffocation — because of the contortions fatties have to go through to come to grips with the situation.

To re-phrase a revolting old limerick:

An 18-stone man from Khartoum
Took a 16-stone girl to his room.
He said, 'Darling — just wait.
'Let's get this thing straight.
'Who does what? And with which? And to whom?

Most sex manuals aren't much help. They may offer 101 variations on a theme, but they've been thought up for people agile enough to get themselves into position in the first place. And to get themselves out of it in the second place.

A double hernia, slipped disc or attack of cramp can take the shine out of any Enchanted Evening. The only precaution you can take is to make love within reach of the phone. Even then, what happens if you dial for help?

'Emergency services. Which do you want: fire, police or ambulance?'

'You don't happen to have a contortionist or all-in wrestler on your books, do you?'

'Oh, it's one of those, is it? No, 'fraid not. But I'll put you through to our heavy rescue squad. Just one word of advice: when they get there, make sure they warm the crowbars first.'

The more thoughtful manuals do offer positions for the overweight, but there aren't many of them: no trampolines or chandeliers for you. And what there are don't exactly add up to sudden and tempestuous passion. By the time you've got in position, you're likely to have forgotten why you're there in the first place. Nor are you likely to be lovingly entwined: in fact you could even be facing opposite directions. ('All right your end, my love?')

Sex aids for the overweight don't figure much in the sex shop catalogues, either. Apart from corn plasters for the shoulder blades, vibrating breeches buoys, block-and-tackle and personalised forklift trucks, there's not a lot anybody can offer.

The *Aaargh!* Factor

One of the biggest obstacles to sex for the overweight is death, from which very few people recover.

('What did your late husband do before he died?'

'He went, "Aaargh!" ')

Even for the fit and slim, sex is a very strenuous activity and puts a sudden, if not totally unexpected, strain on the heart. Imagine doing the same thing carrying two very heavy bags of shopping

(pause to work that one out) and you've got some idea of the extra effort involved for the overweight.

Not only that, the strain is being put on a heart which every day is already working overtime just carting around the equivalent of those two bags of shopping.

Almost all fatal attacks during sex happen to men, which comes as no surprise: they're doing all the acrobatics while their partners are closing their eyes and thinking of England. Most of the potential fatalities have had a heavy night on the town — bags of food and booze — and are making love to women other than their wives. But if you're overweight, you risk its happening during a perfectly normal, run-of-the-mill marital encounter, especially if you've been stuffing your face beforehand.

A summary of advice from heart specialists is:

1. If you can walk up two flights of stairs without palpitations, you should be fit enough for sex. (If they set in on the first flight, don't bother with the second. If they set in on the first *step*, what the hell were you thinking of in the first place?)

2. Go easy on the food and booze beforehand. (Your partner could help here by doing a Lysistrata: if you have a nibble before, you don't get a nibble after.)

3. Use only a position you are used to. (Shouldn't be difficult: it's probably the only one you've got.)

4. Have sex in your own bed, with a familiar partner. (It may take some of the novelty out of things, but at least you can always come back for another go.)

* * *

Running and bouncing are good for your sex life — once your weight's down enough to do it in safety — according to an exercise programme for middle-aged men monitored by the University of California.

The men, aged between 44 and 48, were split into two groups. One group spent 40 minutes a day, for nine months, either jogging or trampolining. The other group walked for an hour a day.

The runners and bouncers reported a much greater increase in their sexual desires than the walkers. They kissed and cuddled more often and their average frequency of sexual intercourse rose from 2.29 to 3.1 times a week. They found also that the frequency of extra-marital sex went up from once every five weeks to once every 3½ weeks.

That must have led to trouble with the end-of-term reports:

'Hi, honey. I've got full marks for our 3.1 a times a week. And an extra star for seeing Lulubelle every 3½ weeks instead of every five. Lulubelle? Oh, she's . . . She's, er . . . Oh, shucks . . . Oh, shit . . .'

Wives whose husbands were in a control group doing marathon running, however, could take comfort. The long-distance runners reported a substantial decline in their sex drives. Though their wives may have spent long evenings looking yearningly at the exhausted figures slumped in the armchairs, at least they knew there was nothing left for Lulubelle.

* * *

Figures for calorie consumption during sex vary from source to source between 125 and 300 or more per session. But as you can burn up 153 calories an hour mending shoes, it's safe to assume that the figures for sex are on the higher side. That would make it the equivalent of an hour's brisk walk, and it certainly isn't so hard on the feet.

In a British chart comparing different physical activities, a figure of eight calories a minute was given for sex. The chart specified that the figures were for activities 'carried out at a moderate speed by normal healthy adults'. No guidance was given, however, on what constituted a moderate speed for sex, nor on how many minutes one should devote to it.

You could time yourself by a metronome or the ticking of the grandfather clock, but that might take some of the magic out of it. There's an element of danger, too: couples have been known to time themselves by the church bell and come to grief when the fire engine has gone past.

To lose a pound in a week would need 12 sessions which, though enjoyable, could be asking a lot of anybody out of practice. But as it also increases the metabolic rate, it almost certainly should shed some more. If it doesn't at least it's fun trying.

In this particular chart, sex scored medium ratings for its contributions to stamina and suppleness (about half that offered by such activities as disco dancing, but what the hell?) and only a low rating for building up strength. Which must come as news to nobody.

Several American consultants have recommended sex as a way of losing weight. One promised a weight loss of 4lb to 5lb a month, simply by substituting sex for the bedtime snack.

'If you're hungry after sex,' he said, 'you haven't done it properly. Do it again.' (All right, then.)

To reach the promised weight loss, however, he advocated 12 extra sex sessions a month, which could prove a little strenuous for those with an already full schedule. ('*Twelve* extra sessions? Bang go my nights off . . .')

To help lose more, he recommended diets based on raw fruits, salads, vegetables and proteins. Plus, if anyone was finding the going a bit rough, some special aphrodisiac meals which included such delicacies as caviar, oysters, crabmeat, clams, frogs' legs, oysters and smoked salmon.

The one snag with the aphrodisiac diet was the expense. At current prices it works out about £35 per day per couple. There are no statistics on how much weight is lost through worry over the cost, or how much weight is put back on from overeating through anxiety about the bills.

One thing for sure is that sex is perhaps the one appetite stronger than that for food. As witness the story of the dumb blonde at the zoo, who was disappointed to find the monkey cage empty.

'It's the breeding season,' the keeper explained. 'They're all in their sleeping quarters making love.'

'Would they come out if I threw them some peanuts?' asked the blonde.

'I doubt it,' said the keeper. 'Would you?'

* * *

Even for slim people, sex is a great aid to keeping in trim. It's best to listen carefully to any medical advice, however. There was the sad case of the thin girl who wanted to gain weight. She took her doctor's advice but began to grow even thinner. Only on her return for a check-up did she realise that she was a little hard of hearing, and that the doctor had not prescribed three hearty *males* a day.

* * *

Should a wife be going off her husband because he's twice the size he was when they walked down the aisle, she ought to look at what she's putting on the table. She feeds him, after all.

A survey in Britain showed that many young husbands start to put on weight shortly after marriage. They are more likely to be overweight than their elders, the opposite of the situation among women.

The cause is the Food of Love. The young wives want to please their husbands, to keep up their strength, to build them up, to show that they can cook equally as well as the mother-in-law. So they dish up far more grub than is needed for the husbands' jobs or lifestyles.

The husbands, in turn, eat up every scrap put before them: partly because they've never had it so good, but also because they want to show their appreciation for the little woman who has spent all that time slaving over a hot stove.

The possibility that a young husband has another woman who is fattening him up is unlikely. Men do not call on their lady loves for food, usually for something that is more likely to take weight off.

There are always exceptions. The author knew one unprincipled husband who had two girlfriends: one was a right raver, and the other was a superb cook. As the weight of the unprincipled husband didn't vary by a pound over the several years he paid court to the two ladies, presumably the efforts of one balanced out the efforts of the other. Some people have all the luck.

Over-eating by young husbands is a very sensitive area for either partner to tackle. If *he* suggests that she puts less before him, *she* is likely to go straight into the slaving-over-a-hot-stove-all-day-and-what's-the-*matter*-with-my-cooking? routine.

If *she* suddenly cuts the quantities or substitutes less fattening menus, *he* is likely to launch into unkind remarks about rabbit food and the observation that although lettuce might do wonders for a rabbit's sex life, it's going to do nothing at all for his.

If they can't work it out by themselves, the only solution may be for the pair of them to visit the Rabbit Guidance Council. (See how it gets you.)

* * *

A mass increase in weight among women villagers in remote parts of Asia was attributed directly to sex. They all lost the weight after nine months or thereabouts, but it didn't make them feel any happier.

A United Nations report to the Asian and Pacific Population Conference in 1982 described how birth control methods had been demonstrated in remote Asian villages. Somehow the message didn't quite get across, and men had been taking the Pill meant for their wives.

Condoms were demonstrated by being stretched over the finger of the lecturer, or on the end of a bamboo pole. The village men nodded their understanding, then dived happily into their huts for some remote Asian connubial bliss — wearing the condom on a finger or sticking it confidently on the end of a pole.

The brighter ones, knowing there must be something more to it than that, boiled the condoms and ate them ('A little more soy sauce next time, perhaps') or swallowed them uncooked and whole ('The worst chewing gum I've ever tasted . . .').

When the United Nations teams returned to check progress, they were confronted by scores of angry and very pregnant women. Presumably the experts are now producing statistics on the sudden increase of husband battering in remote Asian villages.

* * *

Though sex, marriage and even friendship can all be affected by loss of weight, it's not always for the better. A survey by a New York physician among successful slimmers showed that it could bring problems.

Most single weight losers reported that their new look brought them more admirers and a consequential increase in the number of affairs. Great. But a lot of them had grown fat in the first place because of shyness and compensatory eating. The weight went, but the shyness didn't — and by this time there was no camouflage.

'I hate to tell you this, darling, but I'm really terribly shy.'

'No kidding?'

'Yes. By rights I shouldn't even be in bed with you.'

What happens to the shyness after the weight goes and the affairs set in? Presumably there are several options:

(a) Stop being shy. After a few affairs it shouldn't be too difficult.

(b) Stay shy, stay thin, keep with the affairs and carry on blushing.

(c) Stay shy, stay thin and stay sex-starved.

(d) Stay shy, get fat again, and sigh for the good old days of all those affairs.

Several slimming organisations quoted husbands of successful weight losers as saying that it was like having a new woman in bed. If the husbands had been slimming as well, there often *was* a new woman in bed, according to the New York survey.

Newly-thin husbands found that opportunities for extra-marital affairs increased. And the husbands (dirty dogs) were more likely to consider affairs than were their wives. Many of them, however, had the fear that more affairs would put a strain on them emotionally and financially and were not sure whether they ought to risk it.

Presumably if there were no strain involved they'd have leapt in with both feet, to coin an entirely unsuitable phrase. Perhaps they gave the matter some thought and decided to compromise. ('All right, then. Just a little one . . .')

Newly-thin wives, though more active in bed, were less likely to consider extra-marital carryings-on. They tended, however, to become more assertive, i.e. bossy, and not content any more to play the little woman. (The little woman they played when they were large ladies, if you follow me.)

A wife who had always played second fiddle in the marriage, always been willing to follow her husband as he moved from job to job, would suddenly start saying 'No', and would often branch out into a career of her own. Which may have helped the husband decide whether or not to have an affair.

Friends of former fat people resented the weight loss. They would pretend that they were worried about their friends' health — losing all that weight can't have been good for them, etc. But really they were jealous of the new slimline look — and possibly of the new affairs, though they may have found this aspect of it difficult to take in. Hence the ancient and freely adapted Jewish joke:

'Rachael, now that I've lost all this weight, I'm having an affair.'

'I knew the slimming craze wouldn't last. An affair, eh? Who's doing the catering?'

The morals of this are:

1. There's many a new tune played on a slimmed-down fiddle.
2. Inside every fat man there's a thin, rotten, faithless, unprincipled, cowardly old skinflint trying to get out.
3. Inside every fat woman there's a bossy thin one just dying to tell *him* where he gets off.
4. Lose weight — and find out who your friends are.

* * *

Too much weight can be a handicap also to illicit sex: *especially* to illicit sex.

There is no guarantee, for a start, that a strange bed will stand the strain. Some of the romance may go out of a Close Encounter when the female partner is left gazing at the splintered remains of the marital couch and wondering how she's going to explain the damage to her husband when he gets home.

Extra poundage is also a handicap for men in moments of crisis, such as imminent discovery. The traditional urgent instruction — 'Quick! Into the wardrobe!' — loses some of its urgency when to get in means unscrewing the thing first and rebuilding it with a couple of plywood gussets.

Hiding behind the curtains doesn't work, either. Not only is the bulge a dead giveaway, but the hem of the curtain rides up to reveal ten little piggies attached to two big feet. Hiding under the bed is definitely out. And as for jamming a shade over the head and pretending to be a lamp standard . . .

The only recommended way of avoiding discovery, unless you can find a fire escape, is to pull a counterpane over you, curl up on the floor and pretend to be an outsize bean bag.

A fire escape is essential for any exit by window above the ground floor. Drainpipes are no good to anyone except anorexic cat burglars. And pick a window you can be sure of getting through.

Being stuck half in and half out of the usual small bathroom window, especially in a trouserless condition, leaves one vulnerable to any form of physical retribution the aggrieved party may think up. Worse, gives him plenty of time to think. ('Let's see, now . . . Loofah? Loo brush? Potted palm . . .')

Trouserless conditions are common in such situations because extra weight slows down the dressing process. Hasty dressing is often necessary if you are not to take cold, suffer social embarrassment or be the subject of flimsy excuses.

('Oh, darling . . . You're early. I'd like you to meet Mr Smith. He's a visiting consultant from Weight Watchers' Naturist and Bed Testing Branch . . .')

Once out in the street, most of your problems should be over. But if you have been unable to don your trousers, the problems may only just have begun. The combination of trouserless state with an unmistakably portly figure makes identification and pursuit so much easier:

'Foundry Road Police Station. Duty Sergeant speaking. A trouserless man, eh? Could you describe him? Weighs 18 stone? Oh, *that* trouserless man? No problem. Can you call round in 10 minutes?'

How much better would be the trouserless man's chances if he weighed a little less:

'Foundry Road Police Station. Duty Sergeant speaking. A trouserless man? Of medium build? Could you describe him more precisely? Bald head, ginger beard, crossed eyes. Got that, sir. Any other distinguishing features? A four-masted man o' war tattooed . . . where? You sure about that?

'We'll do what we can, but we get so many of medium build. Especially on a Friday night. You know how it is . . .'

* * *

The stolen weekend in an old country inn . . . How romantic: 16th-century beams and a four-poster bed in which, so 'tis said, Henry VIII once plighted his troth and possibly even pressed his suit.

It is embarrassing for 20th-century troth plighters and suit pressers to have the bed caving in, the four posts doling out double helpings of concussion, and mayhap the whole shoot plunging through the 16th-century floorboards to the detriment of the mock Tudor banquet in the dining room below.

The place may well have stood up to the cavortings of Bluff King Hal, even in the company of Anne of Cleves, to whom he referred affectionately as the Flanders Mare on account of her big bum. But in his day the place was new: woodworm, dry rot and death watch beetle had not set in.

* * *

Outdoor sex is not recommended for the overweight. Even the most basic technique — a knee-tremble in a darkened doorway — can be hazardous. In today's congested cities, any large object blocking the pavement or highway tends to be towed away first and questions asked afterwards. It's embarrassing to be towed to the car pound when you've not got a car.

Even with a car, it's tricky. Emergency services get a regular quota of laughs (though they're not supposed to) from calls to rescue well-padded lovers from the backs of cars whose designers did not include delight among the transports they had in mind.

For the lovers, this is not only embarrassing: if the firemen are not extra careful with the acetylene torch, it can be very painful.

Referred to more fully in *How to Avoid Sex* is the case of the girl who was trapped under her 14-stone lover when his back gave out during dalliance in a car in central London. Firemen had to cut the car practically in half to free the couple. Naturally, they comforted the girl on her lover's prospects of recovery.

'Sod *him*!' she wailed. 'How am I going to explain the state of the car to my husband?'

There is less danger of getting trapped on the back of a motorbike, but there's little danger of getting anything on the back of a motorbike, except perhaps a double hernia or galloping pneumonia. Silly to mention it, really.

The top deck of a bus would seem to offer more scope. But two large partners on the same seat can affect the vehicle's centre of gravity, and is particularly dangerous on bends. ('Cause of accident — Sex? You'll have to do better than that, constable. Unless you want to go back to pounding the beat.')

Perhaps the only real scope the top deck can offer is for ancient sex-on-buses jokes such as, 'How far can we go for a pound, Inspector?'

Which leads us neatly into the next chapter. Just as well, before we get to the really revolting sex-on-the-Underground jokes. Such as, 'Is this Cockfosters . . .?'

CHAPTER SEVENTEEN

As Others See Us

Fat is funny, at least to other people. If it weren't, there wouldn't be so many fat comedians. There wouldn't be the jokes about fat people.

Perhaps the main reason that it's funny is that it's funny. To move with any kind of dignity, the fatty has to keep his mind on it all the time. And it shows: there's a self-consciousness in the stately walk which can easily be mistaken for pomposity. People are secretly waiting all the time for the apparent pomposity to be punctured.

When a thin man slips on a banana skin, it's serious. Passers-by rush over, pick him up, dust him down, make sure he's all right. When a fat man slips on a banana skin, it's hilarious. Help is delayed until passers-by have got over their hysterics.

And when the fatty's fancy turns to thoughts of love — Tee-hee! Ho-ho! Har-har! Hyuk-hyuk!

Even trim and athletic people can look soppy in love. When the soppiness is accentuated by a couple of stones of surplus wobble, it's difficult for anyone to keep a straight face.

Sex appeal and size just don't go together — a fact which comedians throughout the centuries have been grateful for.

So we may as well get rid of them all in one go — the jokes about fat people and their relations with the opposite sex. They're cruel, all right, but they always get the laughs (at least, they did when I was a lad — they've been around a long time). Here goes, then:

I say, I say, I say . . .

I'm not saying my wife's fat, but when I carried her across the threshold I had to make three trips.

A drunk made a pass at a 14-stone girl.

'Here, here!' she cried.

'Where, where?' he said.

After only six months of marriage, the girl left her 18-stone husband. She told the divorce court she just couldn't stomach him any more.

As the fat actress said to the fat bishop: 'Thanks for the tip.'

The fat sugar daddy was heartbroken at losing eight stone. She was a beautiful blonde.

Of course, shape isn't everything in romance. Hence the conversation between two girls at the office:

'He's got 30 thousand a year, but he's bald and fat.'

'You mean he's bald and fat, but he's got 30 thousand a year.'

Then there was the fat girl who decided to buy a pair of sexy jeans. She said to the boutique manager, 'May I try on those jeans in the window?'

'I'm afraid not, Miss,' he said. 'You'd never get in.'

'Never get in those jeans?'

'Never get in the window.'

She went to another shop and bought a skimpy dress off the peg. Displaying it later to her catty friend, she said, 'What do you think of my new dress? I bought it on hire purchase.'

'Really?' said her friend. 'And when do you get the second instalment?'

Then she bought a bikini for her holidays.

'Like it?' she asked her friend. 'I got it for a ridiculous figure.'

'You certainly did,' said her friend. 'You certainly did . . .'

On her holiday in Wyoming she went to a barn dance in a taffeta dress and got arrested.

'What's the charge?' asked the judge.

'Rustlin',' said the sheriff.

She could never get it into her head that to wear sexy clothes, she'd have to eat less. She went into a café, squeezed herself behind a table, and ordered a chocolate cake.

'A whole cake?' asked the waitress.

'Of course,' she said.

'You know best,' said the waitress. 'Shall I cut it into six pieces or eight?'

'Better make it four,' she said. 'I'm on a diet.'

After the meal she went into a shop and said, 'I'd like a bra, please.'

'Certainly, madam,' said the assistant. 'What bust?'

'The last one,' she said.

She's taken up disco dancing now to help get her weight down. What a routine. When she gets there, she takes off her coat and pants.

She was always the wallflower at dances, poor thing. One night, a kind friend who was feeling sorry for her approached one of the local likely lads.

'Do me a favour,' she said, 'and dance with Maisie.' (That was her name, by the way: Maisie.)

'You must be joking,' he said. 'She's not my type at all — far too fat. What could we talk about, anyway?'

'All you've got to do is make polite conversation,' said the friend. 'Go on. It'll make her feel ever so good.'

'Oh, all right,' said the boy, grudgingly, and asked Maisie on to the floor.

Within five minutes she had rushed off the floor in tears and locked herself in the ladies' room, howling.

'Can't understand it,' said the youth. 'I was only making polite conversation with her, like you told me to.'

'Well what did you *say*?' asked the friend.

'I only said, "Heck, Maisie, you sweat less than any fat girl I've ever danced with."'

At another dance, the friend tried again. This time she picked on the local Casanova, who really fancied himself.

'Maisie,' she said, 'this is Jason. Have you met before?'

'No,' said Maisie, simpering. 'I've never had the pleasure.'

'And you won't, darlin',' said Jason. 'Don't worry about that . . .'

Eventually Maisie did meet a boy who was attracted to her, even though it was partly out of professional interest: he was a quantity surveyor.

She confided to her catty friend: 'My Jim is so embarrassing. He's going around telling everyone that he's going to marry the most beautiful girl in the world.'

'What a shame,' said her friend. 'After all the time you've been together.'

One night at the disco, one of his pals approached Jim.

'My God,' he said. 'Who's the fat piece over there? The one with the big boobs, enormous backside and legs like oil drums?'

'Do you mind?' said Jim. 'That's my girlfriend.'

'Oh,' said his friend. 'Nice eyes.'

Later on, Jim's pal tried to make it up with him.

'Really striking figure,' he said. 'Just out of interest, what are her measurements?'

'44, 34, 46, 78,' said Jim.

'78! What the hell's that?'

'Dunno,' said Jim. 'But it isn't half a big 'un.'

It's not *only* fat people who are the butt of the cruel jokes: at the other extreme, very skinny people come in for their share. It was even said of Twiggy that she led a very lonely life because she had no bosom friends.

It's possible for any girl to overdo slimming to the point where her good points disappear altogether. After a marathon dieting session, one girl decided to treat herself to a good meal. She chose a very exclusive restaurant and wore a see-through blouse without a bra.

At the entrance she was stopped by the head waiter.

'I'm very sorry, sir,' he said. 'But you can't come in without a tie.'

Then there was the girl who got her share of the lads, even though she was painfully thin.

One day she swallowed a grape and six blokes left town.

Thank you. And goodnight . . .

* * *

Though well-padded women figure as sex symbols in fiction aimed at men — though even there, there's a limit — the well-padded man never figures as a sex symbol in fiction for women. They've enough of that at home, say the publishers.

What the women want is leanness, meanness, steel and whipcord, all that stuff.

Take the standard hero of Romantic Fiction.

His hair is almost always dark; eyes blue, steel grey or dark. (The dark eyes are best for giving 'unreadable' glances, whatever they are. What the hell's the use of glances if you can't read 'em?)

But so far, so good. It is possible to be tubby and still have dark hair and eyes which match up to specification, even to being unreadable on occasion. But after that the fictional romantic qualities don't apply at all to the man in the life of the average lady reader.

The mouth of the Romantic Hero is a bit on the moody, and sometimes mean, side. And hot with it. It's also hard enough to bruise the heroine's lips and any other parts it happens to come in contact with. His lip curls now and again as he behaves in an arrogant manner.

The mouth of our own well-padded hero may look a bit moody at times and be able to work up the odd bit of heat. But seldom does his little fat lip look mean. More sort of amiable if anything, unless he's pouting about its inability to bruise anything. Sometimes his lip will curl, but usually because he's tripped over something in an attempt to behave in an arrogant manner.

The Romantic Hero's chest is tanned and muscular, usually topped by an equally muscular neck, above which juts a firm jaw. His arms and shoulders are similarly muscled and very powerful. He needs all these muscles, first of all to set the heroine a-tremble at the sight, and then to clutch her in an embrace from which there is no escape.

Our own hero's chest is sometimes tanned, and there are muscles in there somewhere. But the general effect is cosy rather than tremble-making. Above the chest rises a shortish neck, though it's sometimes hard to see where it starts, which is topped by two or three double or treble chins. The jaw at one time may have jutted with the best of them, but these days it just sort of nestles.

The hands of the Romantic Hero are lean and strong. Muscular enough to knock hell out of the opposition and pinion our heroine, but also sensitive enough to do a bit of sneaky unbuttoning, soft caressing and the occasional bit of brain surgery.

(Yes, I forgot. The Romantic Hero is often by way of being a genius: captain of industry, brilliant musician, artist or senior medical consultant. Also, blast his steely eyes and muscular bits, usually with blue blood coursing through his veins.)

The hands of our own hero are pudgy and pink, with fingers which would not look out of place in a frying pan alongside a couple of rashers of bacon. Not really much good for knocking hell out of the opposition, even if he could work himself up to it. Not necessarily too bad at the soft caressing, but fumbly with the buttons and certainly to be kept away from anybody's brain cells.

These contrasts, however, are as nothing compared to the waist. That of the Romantic Hero is slim, lean, hard, muscular, lithe, and often compared to a large member of the cat family such as a panther.

The waist of our own hero is round, soft, balloon-like, bulging, overhanging, and often compared to a small member of the whale family, such as a pregnant porpoise.

In the face of all this, is our own hero downhearted? Of course he is. But at least he's real. Slim, lithe, muscular, handsome,

domineering, arrogant and aristocratic geniuses such as abound in novels are very thin on the ground in real life.

Though romantic fiction may help a woman to escape from the dullness or routine of her own life, it can lead her to expect too much in the way of a man. Little wonder so many wives lay down a book entitled *Fiona's Musical Surgeon Phantom Aristocrat Tycoon Lover*, look across at what is snoring on the settee and go 'Yuk!'

But would it work if we had fat heroes of romantic fiction? The least we can do is give it a try. Take a look at this extract from *Beryl's Beau Bert — Back from the Front*:

> Bert leapt from the platform of the No. 19 bus well before the stop. Apologising to the two old ladies he cannoned into — picking them up with old-world courtesy, dusting them down, putting their shopping back in the bags — he set off across the road in pursuit of Beryl, the sight of whose lissom form had occasioned the death-defying leap.

And there she was, standing pensively outside Sainsbury's.

'Beryl! Wait!' shouted Bert. His feet pounded the hard granite pavement, his breath whistled in and out of his agonised lungs, and his heart raced like a mad thing — partly out of passion for Beryl, but mainly because propelling 16 stone a hundred yards at speed from a standing start takes some doing.

Beryl turned at the sound of the familiar voice. But was this *really* Bert? When they parted all those months ago he had not been purple.

'My own dear love!' he cried.

As he did so, the middle button of his jacket — immaculately tailored by King Kong Fashions of Savile Row (Singapore) — pinged off and hit her between the eyes.

This was indeed Bert.

'Darling!' he cried, clutching her to his heaving stomach. 'Darling! It's me — back!'

'Feels more like your front,' said Beryl. And then, as Bert fumbled with the buttons on her cardigan: 'Bert! Not here! Why are you fumbling with my buttons?'

He looked at her, panting. His eyes full of pain and regret.

'They're caught in my braces!' he cried.

'Here, let me,' said Beryl, her slim fingers running sensuously over the reinforced elastic. 'Now then — where have you been these past, long, agonising months?'

'The Foreign Legion. I joined to forget.'

'Forget what?' asked Beryl, lowering her eyes and blushing demurely.

Bert winced.

'After a couple of weeks I was so hungry I couldn't remember,' he said. 'I went down to nine stone and could see no end to the suffering. Then one night it all came back to me — a vision of you behind the counter of your father's high class pie and peas emporium. So I deserted.'

'Darling!' breathed Beryl.

'Yes. For days I wandered the trackless desert, starving and crazed with thirst. I reached the coast a living skeleton and stowed away in the hold of the first ship I could find. As luck would have it, it was sailing for Liverpool.'

'My love!' exclaimed Beryl, her eyes alight. 'And did that mean more agonising weeks of hunger for you?'

'Not really,' said Bert. 'The hold was full of Algerian wine, Turkish delight and crates of salami. That's how I put the weight back on.'

He took Beryl in his arms and crushed her to him. Through the flimsy cable stitch of her cardigan she could feel the pounding of his navel. He pressed his full lips squelchingly on her ear.

'But that's enough about me,' he whispered, fighting down the passions aroused by what he had to say next. 'Let's talk about us. I've something very important to ask you . . . But I'm almost afraid . . .'

'Oh, say it — say it, dearest!' exclaimed Beryl, her eyes brimming with hot salt tears.

'Very well! But by God — it's taking more courage than I thought I had!'

'Anything! Anything!'

'Right, then. Is that job still going at your father's pie and peas emporium . . . ?'

* * *

Yerss . . . It does lack a little *je ne sais quois* . . .

Androcles and the Lion

Androcles was a poor slave in Roman times who had a very hearty appetite. Every spare minute of the day, when he wasn't busy slaving, he would tuck into the buttered dormice and larks' tongues that his master kept for banquets.

He grew fatter and fatter, so that soon there was hardly a toga which would fit him. His master was constantly being embarrassed by having all his guests lying around, waiting for the ante-orgy feast, only to be told that the larder was empty again.

So one day he called Androcles before him.

'Andy, old son,' he said. 'This breaks my heart, but I cannot afford you any more. You will have to go.'

'Please don't send me away, Master,' pleaded Androcles. 'I am very happy here. Besides, I do the work of three men.'

'Perhaps,' said his master, 'but you eat the food of ten. I'm going to count to five, and if you're not gone by then I'll lock you away with no food for a fortnight. Now . . . I, II, III, V minus I . . .'

Androcles knew that his master was a man of his word, so before the final count of V, he was out of the villa as fast as his little fat legs would carry him.

It was a cruel, hard world outside, and Androcles could never get enough to eat. He tried working for several local tradesmen, but his habit of scoffing everything in sight meant that he was never in a job for long. So he took to sneaking back into the villa at night and raiding the pantry.

It was not long before he was caught at it. This time his master had no mercy. He had Androcles sent as ballast in a ship sailing to Africa. From a port on the North African coast, the poor slave was taken into the desert and there left to his fate.

Hungry, thirsty and exhausted, he crawled into a cave and fell asleep. He was awakened by a terrible roaring and was horrified to see, blocking the cave mouth, a huge lion. He had gone to sleep in the beast's den!

He closed his eyes and waited for the lion to strike him down, but nothing happened. Only the terrible roaring of a beast in pain.

He opened his eyes again and saw that the lion kept licking one of its paws and holding it out to him as if it were asking for help.

Moving closer, he saw what the trouble was — a huge thorn sticking out of the paw.

Tenderly he removed the thorn and stemmed the flow of blood. The lion's roars of pain changed to a deep purring sound and it licked his hand in gratitude.

Completely unafraid now, Androcles fell into an exhausted sleep. When he woke up, he found a dead sheep lying by his side. The lion had been hunting and had brought him back a present.

For six months, Androcles lived with the lion in the cave. Every day the lion went hunting and brought back a sheep, which Androcles cooked and ate with relish.

One day, when the lion was out, some Roman soldiers burst into the cave and arrested him.

'What for?' he asked.

'Sheep stealing,' said the sergeant in charge of the party.

'Ridiculous! I've not been stealing sheep. It's this lion that lives with me — '

'Pull the other one, it's got *campaniles* on,' said the sergeant. 'We know all about you, anyway — you're that fat slave who was slung out for guzzling. Well, now it's your turn to be guzzled. You're being sent back to Rome for the Games. They're a bit low on Christians at the moment — the poor lions hardly know where their next meal's coming from.'

Androcles was sent back to Rome in chains, to await the Games on the next public holiday. Sure enough, the time came round, and he was shoved into the arena to await his fate.

As he stood there, watched by the Emperor of Rome and the jeering crowds, a gate in the wall opened, and out sprang a ferocious and hungry lion.

The lion made straight for Androcles, who was about to close his eyes and meet his doom when he realised — the fierce lion was none other than his old friend from Africa, whose paw he had healed.

He stretched out his arms towards the beast.

'Old friend!' he cried. ''Tis I! Androcles! How wonderful to see you again!'

The lion paused, looked up into Androcles's eyes with a glow of recognition, and then bit off his head. It took the lion quite a time to eat the rest of him because, despite his recent privations, Androcles was still pretty tubby.

'That's better,' thought the lion, smothering a burp. 'It's made up for all those sheep I never had. And he got me into this in the first place — I'd never have been here if he hadn't shopped me to the Fuzz . . .'

CHAPTER EIGHTEEN

Seven Deadly Sins

Normally, there's nothing like a spot of sin to take your mind off food. But nobody overweight is in shape for any really enjoyable sinning apart from guzzling. Hasn't got the figure for one thing. Hasn't got the energy for another. Often so slothful that there's not even the inclination.

Even the Good Old Good Ones, the tried-and-trusted Seven Deadlies, have different meanings for the fatty. So conquer those first. Get yourself in trim. Then you'll be ready and willing for some real sinning. And what's more — able.

Pride

Nothing wrong with a bit of real pride. Pride in achievement, pride in appearance. But pride for the fatty is often self-deception: pride which refuses to admit that one is easily led, weak-willed, lacking in moral fibre, greedy, idle and self-indulgent.

You may be too proud to admit, girls, that your ankles are a little thicker than they were a short while ago. That your waist is no longer a waspy handspan. That the fat you can feel above your midriff is a solid layer, and not just a bit of puppy fat pushed up by your belt. That your child-bearing hips are no more child-bearing than they were when they were only half as wide. That your 38-inch bust is a structure of quantity rather than quality, and that its shape owes more to the bra maker's art than to Mother Nature. That your little *gamin* bottom is now of proportions which could be shared between a couple of five-a-side *gamin* football teams.

You may be too proud to admit, lads, that the bulge at your belt is something more than over-developed abdominal muscle. That the spread of your chest is something that deserves support and sympathy rather than admiration. That the biceps which fill your shirtsleeves are only 7½ per cent muscle. That, for all your impressive bulk, you are nowhere near as strong or as fit as you were when you weighed two or three stone less. That you are cheating when you stand in front of the bathroom mirror in Mister Universe poses. You know that the whole magnificent edifice will flop like a mound of melting jelly the moment you breathe out. And you can't go through life just breathing in.

So let's stop kidding ourselves. Let's look at ourselves when we're not looking. As it were.

When you've got over the shock, don't just stand there. Do something. If it's only scream.

Covetousness

Thou shalt not covet thy neighbour's choc ice, nor his cream bun, nor his peanut butter sandwich. Also shalt thou not stand dribbling outside the dwellings of confectioners, nor those of the purveyors of sweetmeats.

For verily is covetousness but one step from laying thy sticky fingers upon temptation. And such is not the way of the righteous. Such is the way of the slob.

Lust

That's a laff. Until you're back in shape, it's not a bit of good lusting. Not unless you are prepared for your lust to go unrequited.

Even should you touch lucky and have it requited by some sympathetic or shortsighted partner, lusting is fraught with danger. Wheezing, shortage of breath, palpitations, hernias, slipped discs and perhaps the occasional attack of apoplexy tend to detract from performance and certainly do nothing for the image.

Most of the great lovers of antiquity were thin. OK, with all that exercise they were bound to be, but they had to be thin to get started. Otherwise you'd have had Romeo crashing to the ground and ruining the balcony scene; Don Juan having to change his name to Don Two; Lancelot's trusty steed buckling at the knees; and Casanova cracking up halfway through the day's quota.

What usually happens to lusting fatties?

A bloke is told that she looks upon him as a brother, a solid and dependable friend, a comforting economy-sized teddy bear in times of trouble. But she has no feelings for him other than those.

If he tries any feeling on his own account, he gets his wrists slapped.

A girl is told that she's great fun. A good sport. Almost — how can he put it? — one of the boys. See you around. Some time.

Boo hoo.

Anger

It's no use getting angry about your lack of success in the lusting stakes. It'll only send your blood pressure up — blood pressure you wouldn't have if you were thinner.

No use trying to sweep out in a stern and dignified exit, either. You'll only bump into something or fall over something. Giving rise to muffled titters which will put you deeper into a tizzy.

Whatever you do, don't let your anger send you to the pub or the pantry for consolation.

Don't fret. Sweat.

Envy

Of course you're envious.

All those friends and acquaintances with good physiques or trim figures. Looking smarter than you, luckier in love, getting about more, having the money to do it. Better off because, apart from the money they'd otherwise spend on cakes and ale and outsize outfits, their trimmer shapes have helped them in the job and promotion stakes.

But don't let the envy get to you. Turn it to advantage. Don't just stand there being jealous of other people's trim figures. Get one of your own.

Gluttony

Now we're getting down to it. The Big One. The cause of most of the trouble.

Gluttony has all the attractions of a sure-fire sin. It's pleasant. It's easy. Apart from money, it needs no special facilities. And you can indulge in public, in company, or in the privacy of your own home. They can't touch you for it.

But be sure this sin will find you out. There's no way of keeping it secret. As sure as the wrinkles on the picture of Dorian Gray, the jellyrolls under your jumper will give you away.

And the temptation is always there. Of course that fruit cake is drool-making. Of course double cream is delicious. You wouldn't find them so hard to refuse if they weren't.

But you're strong, aren't you? You're determined, iron-willed, aren't you?

Of course you're not. But you're still not having any.

Sloth

On your feet. Out of that chair. Away from that telly.

Let's have you out in the garden, working a bit of that fat off. Or padding down the road at a nice brisk pace. Head up, chin in, chest out. Averting the eyes from the food shops. And passing the pubs.

Start your exercise routine today. Now. This minute. Of course you don't feel like it. If you did, you'd be fit, wouldn't you? No excuses — just get the lead out.

Question: How can I lose my fat backside?

Answer: Get off it.

CHAPTER NINETEEN

The Stars in Your Size

If you're seeking excuses for excess weight, it is comforting to think that the reason may lie not in your diet, sedentary habits, glands or gluttony, but in your stars. ('Sorry about my pot belly, Doc, but I've got Scorpio rising.')

Each sign of the Zodiac, it says here in this crystal ball, imparts different mental, emotional and physical characteristics to those born under it.

Taurus, for instance, tends to be thickset and possessed of a hearty appetite (i.e. is a glutton). Leo likes the good life too much to stay thin. Scorpio insists on overdoing everything. Capricorn is naturally skinny and, as the sign tends to be careful with money, is likely to remain so.

Check your birth sign in the following pages and see how it tallies with your physical condition. (If your physical condition is deplorable, don't make your stars the excuse for doing nothing about it. Your birth sign may explain why you are the way you are: it doesn't mean you have to stay that way.)

Of course you don't believe in astrology. Of course you only read your stars for fun. Load of old rubbish, really. Bet this lot rings a few bells, though.

ARIES (March 21–April 20)

The Arien is a muscular type with a fine carriage and a lean, aristocratic profile. To begin with, that is.

He's always in a hurry, which tends to keep the metabolic rate up and the weight down, perhaps well into middle age. His constitution is as tough as old boots. And it can stay that way so long as he doesn't abuse it.

So what does he do? Abuse it. Usually by being too impatient to take any notice of warning signs that he's overdoing things.

When an Arien is hungry, he wants food *now*. This minute. To hell with the diet sheet: what's on the menu? Let's try the dumplings. And plenty of gravy. With spotted dick to follow.

However fast the dumplings are placed in front of him, however quickly they disappear, however lavishly the dick is spotted, he'll complain if they're not up to scratch. In spite of his hurry, he likes his food well cooked and appetisingly served. And, always, lots of it.

Ariens tend to overeat increasingly as they get older, and to ignore the doc when he tells them to cut down. Unless they start eating smaller and plainer meals, the result could be apoplexy. Not to mention six chins, a pot belly and a waddle. None of which does much for the fine carriage and lean, aristocratic profile.

There's also a tendency towards compensatory eating when Aries is not getting his own way, when the going gets tough, or when things are a bit too quiet.

Patience is among the least developed of his qualities and this, combined with his habit of leaping from one unfinished project to the next, makes it difficult for him to stick to any one diet regime for more than a few days.

He tends to suffer from kidney trouble and stomach disorders, both of which may be triggered by overdoing the food and drink. He is also accident prone, increasingly so in later life when a combination of haste and waist can cause him to misjudge size and distance.

Head, face and kneecaps are among the vulnerable areas, and can suffer in crowded restaurants as he lurches out of his seat, catches his knee under the table and butts the tray of hot soups being carried at what the passing waiter thought was a safe distance.

As he gains weight, his range of stomach troubles can extend to include trapping it in a revolving door which up to now he'd always been able to negotiate.

Ariens can look younger, live longer, by keeping an eye on their diet, moderating the booze, and looking where they're going. But they take little notice of any kind of advice.

Don't know why I bother, really.

TAURUS (April 21–May 20)

Taurus is the tubbiest sign of the Zodiac, producing more fatties than any of the others. But it generally suits you.

Taurus has a sturdy build, which is a nice way of putting it, and is inclined towards fleshy features. You are not built for speed. Although you think quickly enough, you move slowly and deliberately.

By nature you're strong and silent, but you can project the laugh-and-grow-fat image because you have a broad, slapstick sense of humour. Mind you, with what you eat, you need it.

You like good, old-fashioned cooking, lashings and lashings of it, and are proud of what you can put away. There's always room for more because over the years your stomach expands to cope with the amounts shovelled down.

'Shovelled' is perhaps the wrong word. You eat slowly and have excellent digestion, so you are seldom troubled with unpleasant after-effects. Your health, too, is generally robust . . . until the weight really piles on and causes such nasties as varicose veins, gout, poor circulation, backache and sprains of your naturally weak ankles.

Often you need to be afflicted before you will even admit you have a weight problem. You're stubborn by nature. It's not you who have spread, it's the clothes which have shrunk. They're making cars smaller these days, doors narrower, that's all.

You are also clad in a hide as thick as a hippo's and almost immune to insult. Even at school, cries of 'Fat Bum!' 'Porker Face!' and 'Wobblychops!' meant only that your classmates were jealous of your sturdy physique.

Not only do you love your grub, you turn to it for consolation when you're off-colour or sexually frustrated. You are seldom off-colour but your sexual appetite matches your size, so you need plenty of consolation even when by normal standards you're doing all right.

You are impressed by size: big cars, big houses, airports, railway stations, wide open spaces. You hate small animals, love big ones. All of which mean that by comparison you appear smaller than you are, at least to yourself.

The sign of Taurus governs the throat, which is the most sensitive organ of your body: possibly because the lining has been worn thin by the constant passage of food.

The best singers are often Taureans. But they spoil themselves by a tendency to sing songs like *Boiled Beef and Carrots, I Get a Kick Out of Stew, A Lot of What You Fancy Does You Good* and *My King-Sized Stick of Blackpool Rock.*

But the Taurean has a will of iron. Once the mind is made up to do a thing, the thing gets done no matter what. If you decide to slim, you slim. All that is needed is the motivation, such as a sudden shock. Highly recommended among sudden shocks is an unexpected glimpse of yourself in a State of Nature.

Check now, if you like. Into the bathroom and off with the motley. Close your eyes and turn to the mirror. Now open them quickly and —

Eeeeek!

Sorry about that . . .

GEMINI (May 21–June 21)

Most Geminis are lucky in having slender bodies, often really skinny ones, being taller than average and having small features. They also have a lot of nervous energy which soon takes care of the occasional overdose of calories.

They are ruled by Mercury, messenger of the gods, who defies all the laws of aerodynamics by flying all over the place with totally inadequate wings on his boots. Geminis are seldom still, rushing here, there and everywhere, exercising their bodies and minds — and most of all their tongues.

They love to talk, which leads them into bad habits such as gossiping, poking their noses into other people's business and spreading scandal. So they're often moving about causing trouble, or moving about trying to avoid the people they caused it for.

Another Gemini characteristic is the dual personality, which at its extremes can be a real Jekyll and Hyde. This, too, helps to keep Gemini on the move — Jekyll rushing around to apologise for what Hyde said the night before.

The contradictory personality can be seen in the rare fat Geminis — the most miserable fat people you've ever seen and the complete opposite of the Jolly Fatty image. They get fat mainly out of boredom. A social rut, routine job or lack of sexual outlets can send them straight to the biscuit tin or junk food emporium to make up for it.

They find it hard to stick to an organised diet. If their erratic reading habits are anything to go by, they'll start with the more tempting meals at the back of the diet sheet: the ones designed for people who have already got their weight down. After a few of those, they'll switch to the lettuce-and-prunes shock-horror dishes at the front, and then give the whole thing up.

It is difficult for a man married to a Gemini woman to regulate his eating. One night the table will be groaning under large and beautifully cooked helpings of everything. Next night she will produce a can of beans.

Gemini women appear fragile, delicate, birdlike and ever so refeened. But the porcelain exterior hides an enormous amount of primitive animal passion. Which comes as a surprise now and again to some unsuspecting but very lucky man — or possibly two or three — and helps to keep the weight down for all concerned.

Queen Victoria was a Gemini, which comes as a surprise to everybody. In later life, certainly, she was no fragile little flower. But that was after Albert had passed on (from sheer exhaustion by the sound of it) and perhaps the dear lady overdid the state banquets as consolation.

The Gemini man, also, is highly sexed. And because of the sign's ability to do two or more things at once, he will often be toying with the affections (and anything else he can reach) of two or more ladies. Again, a social service: like his female counterpart he's helping to raise metabolic rates all round.

Sex apart, however, the men can't stand much pressure. Their normal reaction is to sidestep and move out of the way. But if they're stuck with it — henpecked, say, at home or work — they'll compensate by raiding the fridge and sneaking downstairs at midnight for secret peanut butter orgies. Or they'll go down to the boozer to quaff a few highly calorific pints and boast to their mates about what they told the wife to do with her expensive new curtains.

If the nagging keeps up, they may well leave home. But they're always back in time for tea.

CANCER (June 22–July 22)

Feeling sorry for yourself, are you? Don't worry — it's one of the Cancer traits. Sensitive, moody, brooding, fanciful, timid, fearing for the future and given to the odd wallow in self-pity.

Though only a cruel person would say it, the odds are that you do have something to worry about. (You unfeeling swine, Parker, you.) The pure Cancerian type is big, awkward, ill-proportioned, a tailor's nightmare. Hair looks dull and sparse and the walk is uncertain. Mind you, the pure type can often be modified by other influences, such as Quasimodo rising, so it may not be as bad as all that.

Shyness and persistent worry about the future can cause retreats into solitude, and this often means solitary eating. Food represents security to Cancer. The larder will always be full. Even the wardrobe may contain dozens of tins of food, much of which you are not really keen on, but they were bulk-buy special offers which appealed to your careful attitude towards money.

Cancer hates to waste food of any kind, will clear up everybody else's plate after a meal, and make sure that the leftovers in the pans are turned into bubble and squeak for tomorrow's breakfast. However full he or she may be, food still holds an enormous fascination. When the last mouthful has been forced down, when there's no room for a single spoonful more, it's time to enjoy talking about the next meal.

The appetite is gigantic and the will not over-developed. As if that weren't enough, the stomach is weak and often unable to cope with all that is shoehorned into it.

Cancerians are born actors and will make great theatrical gestures to attract attention: perhaps by stuffing themselves with food for months and swelling up like balloons to emphasise their real or imagined physical unattractiveness.

They are prone to hypochondria and have a tendency to strange fantasies. They will imagine, for instance, that they have chronic indigestion and that their weight has shot up by three stone in six months. And then they'll discover that it's no fantasy.

Now for the good news. And not before time.

Cancerian women are marvellous cooks and will feed up husband, children, relatives and friends like nobody else. The danger here is that the nourishment will be overdone and that the whole family will finish up as candidates for crash diets.

Get a Cancer man or woman into a slimming club and their whole attitude can change. All it needs is a cause. The normally shy, negative Crab will start to organise others, jolly people along into sticking to their diets and exercise routines. And jolly is the word: the pessimism disappears and is replaced by a great sense of humour, a gift for clowning and an infectious belly laugh.

Cancerians have a quality of persistence which enables them to get through the most daunting of tasks, simply by chipping away at the job, bit by bit. Once a diet regime is decided upon, Cancer will stick to it.

Mind you, once target weight has been reached, there's the danger of indulging in a big blow-out to compensate for all the past suffering.

Sometimes it's tough being a crab.

LEO (July 23–August 23)

We've got a right one here. The complete extrovert. Working hard, playing hard, eating hard, drinking hard. Leos are often given to dissipation, ignoring warnings from friends, enemies or doctors, and then wondering why their livers leave home.

Leo is the sign of enjoyment, of pleasures, sports, entertainments, picnics, banquets. The physique is strong, sturdy, robust. It takes a lot to make Leo crack up, but he often does — simply by dedicated pursuit of all the lovely things that are immoral, illegal or fattening.

The 20-stone porpoise wheeled into the health farm with the prunes-and-bran consultant holding one hand and the cardiologist holding the other, is often a Leo.

He can't understand how it happened. His only crime has been years of scoffing and swigging and smoking and late nights and plenty of how's-your-father. I mean, that's normal, doctor, isn't it? Doctor . . . speak to me!

Leo rules the generative organs, the heart and the spine. And if there's a more deadly combination than that, the docs don't wish to know. Excessive activity with the generative organs can cause the heart to pack up in absolute despair. The best you can hope from it is a bad back.

A leader and showman, Leo needs an audience all the time. He likes to prove his success in material terms and insists on nothing but the best. He insists on good cooking, plenty of it, and damn the expense.

If ever he feels himself being ignored, if nobody is paying him compliments, if he feels he's failed in a task or a personal relationship, he marches straight to the nearest pub or restaurant for a few fattening helpings of compensation.

The Leo woman, too, loves the good things in life. When she eats out it has to be at a good restaurant: good food, good service, impressive surroundings, fawning waiters, the lot. She's nobody's for a beefburger and chips.

Though her appetites, like her male counterpart's, are large, she is conscious enough of her good looks to want to keep them. Any over-indulgence is soon corrected.

Her taste in clothes is exquisite and she makes sure she has the figure to show them to their best advantage. She thrives on attention and flattery from men, so she makes sure that the clothes, in turn, are showing her figure to its best advantage.

Meanwhile, back at the health farm, the Leo man is buckling down to his diet. He will buckle down to it if only to prove there's nothing he can't do once he puts his mind to it.

His qualities of leadership and fun find expression in organising glee clubs, cross country teams and patients' concerts. His love of other activities soon becomes evident from the female screams in the massage parlour or the shrieks from the shrubbery during the afternoon ramble.

It's fun being a lion. If you can stand the pace.

VIRGO (August 24–September 23)

You've little to worry about in the overweight stakes, you plodding, predictable old Virgo.

Quiet, hardworking, modest, painstaking, the Virginian doesn't ask much from life. Unadventurous, unheroic, practical, trustworthy, clean, decent, respectable, observing moderation in all things, Virgo is everything a solid citizen ought to be. An example to us all. Ho hum . . .

The physique is graceful, small, spare and wiry, a neat one on which to hang stock-size clothes. The clothes are kept spick and probably span by regular grooming. The general impression is dapper, but without any trace of flashiness.

A true Virgo should have little need to slim. The natural fussiness about food includes almost automatic counting of calories, carbohydrates and vitamins. The diet is often a health food one, and may even be vegetarian. There won't be any madly exotic dishes, nor is the range likely to be great. Virgo is a creature of habit, knows what he or she likes, and sticks to it.

Meals are cooked to the second: you'll never find a Virgo burning the joint, or even the toast. The kitchen will be scrupulously clean: dirt means germs and Virgo hates both, especially germs which could upset the delicate stomach. (Not that the upset would last long: Virgo keeps enough pills, potions and lotions to stock a chemist's.)

Portions are carefully measured. The meals are enough to fill: no more. Virgo does not hold with blow-outs. As well as being bad for you, they cost money.

Though Virgo may suffer the occasional stomach upset or bout of indigestion, it's usually caused by worry rather than wrong eating. The diet includes enough roughage to keep things moving and Virgo takes the recommended amount of exercise to help the digestion along and keep the body in trim.

The regular lifestyle helps digestion, too. If Virgo goes to the loo at 7.30 a.m. and 8.30 p.m. on Mondays, Virgo will go to the loo at those same times every day of the week. A Virginian caught, say, on a motorcoach with no toilet will feel decidedly ill at ease once the time has passed, and may even ask the driver to pull up at the first convenient convenience. Blushingly, of course.

When Virgo does let things slide, it's often because of materialistic insecurities. Virgo has a fear of debt and worries a lot about money, either getting it or keeping it. The pursuit of money may lead to long working days and perhaps late-night budgeting operations. This can cause neglect of physical fitness routines and to unthinking snacks between meals or in the small hours.

Fat does not look good on the small frame, however, and the sight of the once trim body turning to flab soon forces a return to regular habits. Apart from that, excess weight could mean new clothes, and more expense.

Alcohol is seldom a problem. Not only is it fattening and costly, it can lead to temporary loss of control, and that's foreign to Virgo's precise and prudish nature.

Sex isn't much help as a slimming aid. With sex, as with food, Virgo tends to take just enough and no more.

Their quiet, frugal lives, regular habits and natural good health ensures that Virginians live to a ripe old age. Or if they don't, it feels like it.

LIBRA (September 24–October 23)

A bit of weight can suit the pleasantly rounded Libran. It goes with the sunny, smiling approach to life and provides the famous dimples. (You can always tell Librans by the dimples. Depends on how well you know them, of course: they have dimples in some funny places.)

The sign can run to fat quite easily. First, it's got a good start. Second, Libra believes that nothing succeeds like excess and is happy to overdo the more pleasant things in life such as eating, drinking and making love.

The Libran's love life is quite something, from all accounts, and may help a lot to keep the shape merely pleasantly plump and prevent those dimples disappearing beneath folds of blubber. But a romantic setback can trigger off a bout of heavy eating and boozing. Often it doesn't last more than a few weeks — it seldom takes Libra long to find a new love. But if the bout should be a long one, that new love may have to be looking for a 20-stone sex maniac.

The strange thing is that Libra is forever seeking harmony, a balance. But, true to the sign of the Scales, the balance only happens now and again: the rest of the time is spent moving up and down.

At the point of balance, Libra is calm, rational and charming. Let the scales start moving, however, and he can become quarrelsome, tactless, stubborn and confused.

He never loses his charm, though. Even overweight he's appealing: the archetypal Happy Fatty. He can hand out the most outrageous insults, but utter them with such a sweet smile that the insultee blushes under the hail of what he thinks are compliments.

'Hi there, you slug-brained old moron! Still beating the wife and fiddling the accounts?'

'Why, yes. How nice of you to remember . . .'

Libra is great at giving out gratuitous advice, but among the world's worst at taking it. He'll soon tell you that you're horribly overweight, what's wrong with your diet, and how you ought to go about cutting down on the food and booze. Perhaps all the time cheerfully patting the jellyroll hanging over his own belt.

He loves an argument, too, just for the sake of arguing. Automatically he takes the opposite side to anybody. Tell him you're on a fibre diet and he'll rave about the virtues of pineapple. You mention your pineapple diet and he'll rave equally about the virtues of fibre.

Artistic and sensual by nature, he loves painting, music, good food, fine wines, stimulating conversation, and doesn't stint on any of them. He is also lavish with money, and for his dinner guests nothing but the best is good enough.

The biggest threat to his health is over-indulgence. He loves sweet things, which can bring on excess weight, stomach trouble and bad skin. Booze, too: which can leave him with more weight, kidney and bladder trouble, not to mention a liver with knobs on. Stomach ulcers can trouble him, caused not so much by worry as by asking too much of the stomach.

The strange thing is that Librans are usually healthy: a bout of excess and perhaps overwork can be followed by an equally intense bout of temperance and relaxation.

Temptation is often put in their way because they are in great demand at parties. Their sunny natures, genial appearance and lively conversation guarantee this. Small parties are preferred: Libra suffers from claustrophobia and hates crowds — even to the extent of leaving a packed restaurant before the last course.

Another thing he hates is making decisions. Faced with a choice of two dishes at a buffet lunch, he'll hum and ha for a while, then solve the problem by taking both of them . . . and that's another dimple gone.

SCORPIO (October 24–November 22)

Though Leo and Libra do pretty well in the excess stakes, they can look tame alongside Scorpio. Whether it's food, drink, tobacco, work, play or sex, Scorpions will have too much of it. They excel at overdoing things.

Scorpions, in fact, excel at everything: just you ask them. The sign insists on being the boss. Things will be done their way or done their way. For Scorpions there is no alternative. Any opposition is trampled underfoot. Things *will* be done their way — and that's an end of it.

Both sexes have to watch their weight, not only because of

appetites verging on the gluttonous, but because the Scorpion physique lends itself to bigness.

Scorpio men tend to be thickset and physically powerful, though not particularly tall. The face tends to be dark with a strong jaw and a strong, harsh or even coarse mouth.

An appropriate nickname would be Mafia Mush, not that anybody would say it in Scorpio's hearing, except perhaps Sagittarius. Saggy is not noted for tact, but even the most tactless would only say it once. A couple of weeks in intensive care works wonders for the social graces.

The Scorpio woman gets a better deal, which is not difficult. Though she is often big boned, she has a voluptuous figure, an oval face and a sensual mouth. She, too, has to watch the appetite if those pneumatic curves are not to balloon into . . . what's the word? . . . the things that curves balloon into? Balloons.

Because Scorpions are always right, any suggestion that perhaps they need to lose weight is likely to be ignored. OK, so you're the doctor. What the hell do doctors know about it? Who asked *you*, anyway?

The sign has some morbid and even self-destructive tendencies. So when disappointed, thwarted or perhaps even upset at being told he's overweight, Scorpio may hit the bottle. This could add a few more pounds, so he'll hit the bottle again to get over that. Because he won't admit weakness or even unhappiness, it's up to those close to him to diagnose the problem and work out ways round it: sympathetically, of course, and tactfully, if you don't want a fat lip.

Not that the sign overflows with sympathy for anybody else, or uses much tact, either. Don't ask advice of a Scorpion unless you can face the truth, or at least Scorpio's version of it. Say, 'I'm very worried about my weight. I'm feeling absolutely gross,' and Scorpio will reply, 'So you should be worried. And what do you mean — *feeling*? You *are* absolutely gross.'

Don't expect him to apologise, either, even in the cack-handed Sagittarian way. If he's said it, he meant it. And no way will he retract.

One thing which may get Scorpio on to a slimming regime is his interest in the workings of the human body, and his almost morbid interest in death. Once he realises that his gluttony is upsetting his body mechanism, and may even shorten his life, he'll do something about it. It was his idea, wasn't it? So that's OK by him — and it better be OK by everybody else.

Not that he's afraid of death. Scorpio is afraid of nothing. He just doesn't want it to disagree with him, that's all.

SAGITTARIUS
(November 23–December 21)

Sagittarians are among the lucky ones. They're often tall, graceful, muscular and athletic, which gets them off to a good start. They tend to love sports, travel and the outdoors and combine this with a restless, inquisitive nature which keeps them constantly on the move.

All of which, plus a healthy appetite for sex, keeps the metabolic rates up and the pounds down, in spite of equally healthy appetites for food and drink.

Saggies are born optimists and tend not to fret for long. And because they're usually self-sufficient, they don't get over-dependent on others. So any weight they may put on doesn't come from compensatory eating.

In middle age, however, when active sport gives way to watching from the sidelines or the armchair, the trim waist can start to spread (especially if Saggy has taken up regular boozing, an activity which often appeals to him).

It doesn't take a lot of exercise to get back into trim, however: walking instead of taking the car, climbing stairs instead of using the lift, a country walk instead of watching the afternoon TV movie — that kind of thing is often enough.

Oh, and saying 'No' in the pub to one for the road. That is often difficult. Not only does Saggy like his ale, he's also very sociable and doesn't like to upset people by refusing their hospitality.

Not that he doesn't upset people. He's as tactless as Scorpio, except that he doesn't mean to be.

'Hi there! I hear you're going on a diet,' he says to some poor soul who's been denying him or herself all the good things in life for the past six months and has lost a stone or so. 'When do you start?'

On being told of the poor soul's suffering, he tries to make amends:

'Of course. Yes, I can see it now. You certainly have lost a bit. It must be that suit/dress you're wearing that makes you look fat. And when I first saw you, your head was turned away and I got you in profile. Shows off your double chin, that does. Remember it when you get your photograph taken.'

As the other turns redder and redder with rage or embarrassment, Saggy tries again:

'Yes, of *course* you've lost a lot of weight. Well done. I'd forgotton how fat you were. Last time I saw you, you really were *enormous*. My, my. Just a minute — where are you going . . .?'

Saggies don't put much store by money and are easily conned. So they may well find themselves paying through the nose for a course at a health farm or upmarket slimming clinic when they could achieve the same results much cheaper by attending a less pretentious slimming club or sticking to a proper diet-and-exercise regime at home.

The sign is a healthy one — apart from a tendency in later life to rheumatism, sciatica and blood pressure — and Saggies who look after themselves tend to make quite old bones.

One big threat to their health and longevity is their accident proneness. They are vulnerable in the shoulders, arms, hands, lungs, liver, hips, bowels and feet. Which doesn't leave a lot else to be vulnerable in. And of course, the larger they are, the bigger the target area those things offer. So it pays to cut down the risk by staying slim.

Another reason for staying slim is to ensure a swift take-off speed after a social or domestic *faux pas*. Apart from their natural tactlessness, Sagittarian men are seldom completely domesticated. There is a high incidence of head injuries from such instruments as rolling pins and frying pans wielded by their ever-lovings. It could arise from such a simple oversight as taking a health-giving country walk, but failing to plan it to avoid temptation. How was *he* to know that there were five pubs along the route?

CAPRICORN
(December 22–January 20)

Capricorn men and women both love their homes and, unless it's to further a business deal, prefer eating in. Not only is the food more wholesome — a Capricorn man, even if he doesn't cook, will insist on it — it's a lot cheaper.

The Capricorn woman is an excellent cook. She makes a meal an occasion, with a properly laid table, place mats, napkin rings and even a candlestick or two. But there's no fuss about the food or the menu: both are good, plain and balanced.

Diets are properly planned for all the family, right down to the cat. Everybody is well fed, but none is likely to run to fat on mother's cooking — even though she does insist on them finishing every last mouthful.

Nobody's likely to get food poisoning, either: the kitchen is as gleaming and spotless as the rest of the house.

Generally there's not much flesh on a Capricorn. More fat on a chip, as they say. The bones tend to be large, so what software there is doesn't go very far. This, combined with an angularity of physique, sometimes makes the Capricornian look like an assembly from a kit of spare parts.

Capricornians are very careful and precise in the use of money. They also have an austere streak and can exist on very little, so excess weight is not a problem unless they start to worry. When they *do* start to worry, they make a job of it. Their pernickety, nit-picking natures can make them worry even about having nothing to worry about. ('It's too quiet. What's the matter . . .?')

They will either cut down on expenses which have already been pared to the bone, or they will despair of ever making ends meet and dive straight off into a depressive riot of guzzling.

So you have an instant guide to your state of mind. If you look like a kit of spare parts, you're OK. If you are rattling around like a skeleton on a tin roof, you worry too much. If you are waddling about like a 16-stone ruptured duck, you worry too much. Stop it.

Worry apart, there's little to worry about. Capricornians are steady, plodding climbers, keen to get on in the world and methodical in going about it one step at a time. They are creatures of habit and routine: qualities which can bring on compensatory eating in non-Capricorn spouses from sheer sexual frustration.

There's a fixed time and place for everything; eating, sleeping, cleaning, laundering, shopping, accounting — and sex. So an amorous spouse, eager for a bit of the action, may be told: 'Not tonight, dear — it's Thursday.'

AQUARIUS
(January 21–February 19)

Aquarius puts all the other signs of the Zodiac to shame. He's the supreme idealist, has the highest standards and purest motives of any of them. Makes you spit.

He seldom has a weight problem. The physique is naturally graceful and, though he likes his grub, prefers a little food, well-cooked from the best ingredients, rather than lashings of anything second rate.

Aquarius likes to entertain a lot, however, and can put on extra pounds by joining friends in a treat. A check on generosity can be a sudden shortage of cash: he's a sucker for picking up the tab in a restaurant, even if somebody else is supposed to be paying for the meal.

The main cause of excess weight is the odd bout of over-eating caused by frustration with people or situations which do not come up to the high Aquarian standards. The only way to cure this is by accepting the fact that nobody's perfect, or by keeping away from bores, loudmouths and nasties. He could always take his mind off things by polishing his halo, but he's too modest to realise he's wearing one.

The extra weight seldom lasts long. Aquarius is honest enough to admit the presence of a spare tyre and purposeful enough to do something about it. Certainly there'd be no cheating by trying to disguise the flab with larger or more flattering clothes.

Concern for other people makes Aquarius a good friend to anyone who is overweight. Or underweight: he's aware enough and sensitive enough to understand the problems which can lie behind a condition such as anorexia. There will be no preaching, no blame and certainly no laughing. But, by constructive and subtle suggestion, practical help and example, the friend will be set on the road to a better shape.

If you're cooking for an Aquarian, incidentally, don't let him do the shopping. The sign denotes the original absent-minded professor. He'll come back from the shops with all sorts of things: a screwdriver, a Chinese kite, half a dozen coconuts and a toy plastic submarine. The steak? Oh, you wanted steak . . .?

The Aquarian's food has to be spotlessly prepared if you want to avoid bringing on one of his phobias. A caterpillar on the lettuce, however small and cute looking, could send him rushing to the loo for a panic-stricken throw-up. The food has to be carefully chosen, too, because of his allergies. You could make a beautiful prawn dish and discover that prawns bring him out in a rash. Then you discover that he doesn't like prawns, and that his allergies usually consist of things he's not keen on anyway.

Liberal and misty-eyed dreamer though he is, the male Aquarian has definite ideas about a wife's duties: i.e. she's got to be able to cook.

The Aquarian woman is not exactly noted for her domesticity. She'll have a go at cooking and can turn out some really original dishes. Original is the word. She's highly inventive and will experiment with everything in the larder, but this approach has its drawbacks. She seldom follows a recipe to the letter and likes to add her own particular twist. You may be served Baked Alaska with a slug of Worcestershire sauce in it, just to liven it up.

And imagine getting home from a hard day in the Concrete Jungle to be greeted with: 'Something special tonight, darling. I thought we'd try the kippers with custard for a change.'

You'd have no weight problem there, and that's a fact.

PISCES
(February 20–March 20)

The sign of two fish swimming in opposite directions symbolises the nature of Pisceans. They never know whether they're coming or going, and sometimes aren't all that sure where they've been.

Cheerful, laughing, sensitive, artistic, sympathetic, friendly, attractive. That's the Piscean. Deceitful, artful, devious, secretive, undependable, born liar. That's the same one.

But Pisceans deceive themselves as well as others, and often don't realise when they're fibbing. Anyone who taxes a Piscean with bending the truth gets such a plausible, complicated and long-winded cxplanation — the gift of the gab is another trait — that he comes away ashamed of doubting in the first place.

Though Pisceans in the main are a slim lot, and the women usually stay slim, the men tend towards self-indulgence and some may reach middle age well over riding weight. They can't understand it. Appetite like a bird. Never touch bread, potatoes, biscuits. And always take plenty of exercise.

The culprit may be the Demon Drink. Pisces is a water sign, and people born under it tend to be connected with fluids in one way or another. Some sail the seas, some sell or make chemicals, oils, beverages. Some booze.

A lot of booze, in fact. And this is one of the prime causes of excess weight. Pisceans, you see, are sensitive. Often misunderstood. Accused of fibbing, secrecy, unreliability. Nagged at. Their poetic natures are horrified by the actualities of the world in which they find themselves. So they take to the bottle for consolation. Not a lot, you understand. Hardly ever touch it. Medicinal purposes only. Moderation in all things, that's my motto. Another? Don't mind if I do. Not a word to the wife, old son.

Those born under the sign often won't admit to being overweight, even when confronted by such damning evidence as bathroom scales shattered beyond repair.

'See that?' says Pisces, stirring the wreckage with a big fat foot. 'Made in Taiwan. What do you expect from foreign rubbish?' Then gets dressed and waddles down to the true-Brit weighing machine outside the chemist's which has been registering three stone under any given weight since 1947.

Confronted with a full-length wardrobe mirror, which won't take in his full width at close quarters, Pisces complains that the glass is starting to warp. In the Hall of Mirrors at the fair, he keeps going back to the one which reflects human skeletons, convinced it's the only true likeness in the place. Opposite the one real mirror, he claps his hands over his beer belly and laughs like crazy.

'Just look at this!' he chortles. 'What will they think of next?'

Pisceans are always jumping on to new bandwagons, following one craze after the other like a demented Mr Toad. They will try to counter weight problems by diving straight into the latest diet or exercise fad, stick to it fanatically for three days, and then try something else. No fad is too nauseating or way-out. Anything from drinking 12 pints of celery water a day to swallowing a cupful of frog bile at every meal.

If ever you are in need of secondhand exercise equipment, look in a Piscean's attic. Chest expanders, dumb bells, rowing machines, punchbags, skipping ropes, chinning bars, Indian clubs. All of it in immaculate condition because none of it was used for more than a week. The owner of all this, meanwhile, is bouncing up and down the lawn on a pogo stick — the *only* way to get the weight down . . . this week.

CHAPTER TWENTY

Ve Heff Vays . . .

Some people become so fat, are such obsessive and secret eaters, have such a weird metabolism, have so little willpower — or are just so bloody awkward — that strong measures have to be taken to get their weight down.

The function of this chapter is to examine some of the more drastic methods of slimming which have been tried over recent years.* It is also to get rid of the ancient and revolting slimming joke:

'Doctor, how can I lose 12 pounds of ugly fat overnight?'

'Simple, madam. Just cut off your head.'

The joke has been going the rounds since the French Revolution, when the aristos were trimmed down by a couple of thousand kilos a week. Not one of them said thanks.

Truth, as always, is stranger than fiction. One man whose extra weight did nothing for him at all was Zhang Ziping, a 35-year-old Chinese peasant. He'd have been quite a good-looking bloke if he hadn't had two heads.

The second head grew on the right side of his skull and had sealed eyes, eyebrows, eyelashes, teeth and a beard. It didn't have a lot of brain, though it used to make corresponding movements when the official head ate, frowned or whistled. Which wasn't bad, considering.

The extra weight affected Zhang's social life in that prospective friends or partners used to run away screaming. In 1980, by which time he was getting a bit fed up with prospective friends or partners running away screaming, he talked his father into letting him go to hospital, where the spare head was removed.

When last heard of, he was looking for a wife. See what you can do when you try?

Lock Up Your Molars

The lockjaw treatment is simple and has grown increasingly popular over the last decade.

* Fib-and-fantasy spotters can look for the one method which hasn't — at least in its basic form — been tried yet. Meanwhile keep away from slimming clinics which have any ties with the South Orinoco.

The jaws are wired or cemented together and the slimmer fed a low-calorie diet through a tube. After seven months or so, as much as 100lb can be lost.

It has the obvious drawback of affecting the speech. It may or may not be significant that most of those given the treatment have been women. And it may or may not be significant that there have been few, if any, objections from husbands. In fact several husbands asked if the lips couldn't be stuck together as well: just to stop them flapping up and down and looking untidy.

Some husbands who volunteered their wives for the operation were turned down on the grounds that a woman of eight stone could hardly be considered obese.

It may or may not be significant that several hundred wives did not make the expected weight loss and had to be kept clamped up and silent for longer. Reasons for the disappointing performances may have been that several hundred husbands had worked out a formula for a high-calorie liquid diet. Or simply shoved chips down the tube.

It may or may not be significant that more than a few husbands contacted the hospitals to see if the mother-in-law couldn't be done as well. On a more permanent basis.

Another reason for the preponderance of women may be the reluctance of men to have their social life interfered with by the drastic modification of speech.

It is embarrassing to stand in a pub asking for a Gottle o' Gear or a Gint o' Gitter. And try shouting 'Taxi!' It comes out as 'Thackthi!' Causing insensitive bystanders to shout 'Hello, Thailor!' And leaving you standing cabless on the curb muttering 'Thyit . . .'

The Tapeworm Treatment

American doctors have had spectacular results from administering a tapeworm egg and letting the beastie grow inside the patient, absorbing nourishment and so keeping its host thin. Revolting, isn't it?

When the patient has lost enough weight, the tapeworm is got rid of, or sometimes bits of it are simply cut off to reduce its intake. Don't ask how it is coaxed out into the light of day, or from whence it emerges. (*He-ee-re Blu-ue . . . You good worm, you . . .*)

The treatment has one or two drawbacks, apart from not being the kind of slimming story you can tell at dinner parties. (Correction: The treatment costs so much that no wormhost can resist telling it. At least it puts all the others off their pud.)

When the tapeworm has gone, the patient is left with only willpower, and may turn up six months later, fat as a barrel and with a writ for *habeus wormus*.

There is the emotional problem, too. Some people grow very fond of their tapeworms. Give them pet names and talk to them in baby talk. 'Oo's an ickle-wickle squirmy-wirmy, den? Oo's mama's ickle cheeky face?' And when the time comes for the tapeworm to leave, it's like having the cat put down.

Expelled and defunct but much-loved tapeworms have been causing problems at pets' cemeteries, where graves 24ft long and ¾in wide have played havoc with the ground plans.

A suggestion from the Animal Morticians and Embalmers Federation, that perhaps the dear departeds would be just as happy coiled up and buried in boot-polish tins, met with such a stormy reception that the Federation's chairman was forced to resign on the spot. He is now an embittered and deeply sulking recluse, hoping vainly for a comeback with his plans for burying them above ground by nailing the coffins vertically to telegraph poles.

Pruning by Piranha

Inspired by the success of the tapeworm technique, the Brazilian dietician Senor Pedro Drastiquez experimented further with the use of living organisms as agents of weight reduction.

The tapeworms, though effective, took their time. Speed and simplicity were what Senor Drastiquez was looking for.

He found both with his piranhas-in-the-bath technique. Fifty piranhas in a bath of lukewarm water, in which the patient was immersed.

'Nothing could have been simpler,' said Senor Drastiquez in his address to the South Orinoco Swift Slimmers' Club. 'Nor more effective. My beloved mother-in-law lost 18 stone in half an hour;

my bank manager lost 16 stone in 20 minutes; my local tax inspector lost 14 stone in 15 minutes.

'There were, admittedly one or two unforeseen and unfortunately irreversible side effects, but once I have discovered how to make the piranhas stop in time, all will be well. The most I can do until then is posthumously to salute these three brave people for their contributions to science.'

Senor Drastiquez will be unable to continue his experiments until he has finished the court sentence imposed for assaulting his wife.

'It was all her fault,' he told the jury. 'She refused to get into the bath.'

The Shiver Giver

A Canadian specialist achieved weight losses of a pound a day on volunteers who spent up to three hours daily in a refrigerated room.

The theory was sound enough: you eat food to keep warm. When you're cold, you burn up calories.

'People could do this at home,' he said.

The snag about shivering at home is the cost of converting the average room into the equivalent of a meat vault. Less well-off fatties would be forced to seek a substitute. British fire brigades are reported to be fed up with having to keep prising people out of fridges.

Short Circuit

An operation carried out extensively in the United States is to short-circuit the bowel by removing a length of intestine and joining the two ends up again. This causes the body to absorb only enough food to keep alive.

Everything is worked out to fractions of an inch. Not enough intestine left would mean not only that you starved to death, but that you finished up as a round-shouldered corpse.

Feeling Swell

A technique developed in Denmark involves inserting a balloon in the stomach, pumping it up, and leaving it there. The balloon reduces the stomach's capacity by a third and makes it feel fuller. Eventually the balloon loses air, dissolves or finds its own way out, and is replaced by another.

A variation of the operation in America is to sew the balloon into the body next to the stomach and insert a valve near the navel. The size of the balloon can then be altered, reducing it when the target weight has been reached.

So far there have been no reports of leaks causing the slimmer to go 'Pppppppprrrrrrrpppppppp . . .' into the wild blue yonder, nor, thankfully, of any exploding through over-vigorous pumping. But when it happens, what a story:

Dateline New York

Waldo Fatropp, 46-year-old international financier, gourmet and all-round bon viveur, died in Mount Zion Hospital today after exploding in the Rockefeller Plaza.

He had just left a 12-course charity luncheon in aid of the Profits From The Third World Foundation, and had stopped on the way to his limousine to adjust the valve on his Self-Denial Slimming Balloon.

Windows in the Rockefeller Centre, and for hundreds of yards along Fifth Avenue and 49th Street, were shattered by the blast.

Mr Fatropp was rushed to Mount Zion, but failed to survive simultaneous operations in wards 7, 8 and 9.

He was noted for his post-luncheon fitness routines. He always had the limousine parked at least 50 yards from any business meeting and insisted on walking to it, rain or shine, unless the weather was against it.

He leaves a widow, five mistresses and a dozen sorrowing restaurateurs.

Rub-a-Tub-Tum

A Chinese acupuncturist in San Francisco recommended rubbing fat away — an ancient Chinese technique 6,000 years old.

All you do, he said, is to spend two minutes a day gently massaging the midriff. By the end of a week you could have lost up to 5lb of flab.

You place the palm of the hand on the navel — assuming, in the case of larger stomachs, that your arms are long enough — and with a gentle brushing action rub clockwise in tight circles. Expand the circles until the whole of the tum has been covered, then go into reverse and rub back towards the navel.

'Codswallop,' was how a British dietician described the technique, but at least it can't do any harm. Unlike the method used by the legendary Chinese philosopher who decided that the key to slimming lay in the navel itself. Unscrew that, he thought, and you'd get to the root of the problem.

He inserted a screwdriver in his navel and turned it gently anti-clockwise. After five minutes, his backside fell off.

Suck It and Chuck It

A technique developed in France is Aspiration — removing blubber by vacuum-cleaner surgery. It is used to remove hard, seasoned fat — up to 4lb in one operation — and to re-shape bulgy bottoms and outsize thighs.

The fat is first dissolved with an enzyme injection, and then sucked out into a jar for disposal. Great care is doubtless taken to make sure the vacuum equipment is properly connected — if it blew instead of sucked it would give a new meaning to Getting Your Own Back. All you could do then to even things up would be to turn the other cheek.

Cutting to the Quick

A revoltingly drastic technique, but one which gets instant results, and naturally was developed in America, is apronectomy. The subcutaneous fat around the abdomen is simply cut away in one great chunk.

This technique has been hailed by conservationists as a way of saving the Blue Whale from extinction. The blubber removed by apronectomy, they argue, could be recycled instead of just being left on the operating theatre floor for people to slip on.

One rehabilitation problem caused by the operation is loss of balance. People who have been walking around for years with four or five stone of blubber in front of them tend to leap out of bed with an athletic cry of 'Wahaaay!' And fall flat on their backs.

Skin Tight

A bigger and more long-term problem with apronectomy is what to do with all the spare skin. If it is left on, it flaps about and doesn't look too good in a bikini. If it is cut off and thrown away, trouble can arise later for patients who put the weight back on. After a while, the remaining skin will stretch no longer and patients are in danger of exploding.

One brilliant solution, albeit with only local application, was devised by Mr Hamish MacSlasher, known affectionately in medical circles as The Claymore Kid. At his surgery in Aberdeen he developed a technique of pleating the spare skin after first tattooing it with a clan tartan. This was very popular among Scottish patients as it cut their kilt bills to nothing, though some of them complained that their sporrans tended to tickle.

Another technique which achieved wider popularity was that of Sir Timothy Turnup, later dubbed the Demon Barber of Harley Street. He cut the skin into manageable strips and put it in curlers. If the patient later put on weight, the skin could be unrolled, ironed out and put back in place.

The first few skin replacements went without a hitch, but problems arose later with patients who had taken several years to reach replacement size and whose active lifestyle had detrimental effects on the surplus skin.

After her operation, Miss Booboo ('Every Time She Bumps She Bounces') Rollaball made a comeback in her old profession as an exotic dancer. For a gimmick, she painted the strips of skin green and let them hang down as a grass skirt for her big Hawaiian number. Alas, over the years the ends became frayed: after the replacement there was only enough left for a ra-ra skirt which hardly covered her confusion.

Another patient grew tired of the curlers and instead used setting lotion to keep the curls in place. Days of valuable time were lost before her skin reinstatement operation while the British Museum was scoured for the experts who did the ironing out of the Dead Sea Scrolls.

The most famous technique of all was that devised by Sir Albert Trotter, the self-taught surgeon who started his working life in Lancashire as a black pudding filler.

'It were no fret fer me, lad,' Sir Albert told a television interviewer. 'Me being used to th' problems wi' black puddings when th' filling ran short. We just pulled th'skin tight and tied a knot in the top of the pudding.

'Any road, that's what I did to this young feller after th'operation. Pulled all t'spare skin to th'top of his yed and knotted it. "Yer'll be all right," I said to him, "so long as yer keep yer cap on".'

Life thereafter for the patient, Mr Eli Down, went back to normal. Apart from having to keep his cap on all the time and walking with a slight stoop — the result of Sir Albert's having knotted him a little vigorously — he was as active as ever.

Mr Down was very embarrassed, however, at a Press reception in London held by Sir Albert to demonstrate the results of his operations.

Halfway through the reception, Eli was approached by a lady journalist who wasn't focusing too well after the lavish hospitality poured out by Sir Albert.

'Excuse me,' said the journalist, 'but that's a really cute dimple in your chin.'

'That's not a dimple,' said Eli. 'That's me navel.'

'Is it really?' said the journalist. 'Fascinating. Tell you another thing — I dig that kinky tie . . .'

CHAPTER TWENTY-ONE

And Another Thing . . .

Don't worry. It's nearly over now.

No more preaching. No more lecturing. No more bullying. No more frighteners to bring you out in a cold sweat.

Thanks for staying the course this far. Unless you've merely skipped straight to the end, in which case you're chicken.

By now you will have taken in the Message, and will have solemnly sworn that from this day forward you will:

1. **Eat less.**
2. **Move more.**

It's not a lot to ask, is it?

Pardon?